Men-at-Arms • 548

Armies of the First Sino-Japanese War 1894–95

Gabriele Esposito • Illustrated by Giuseppe Rava

Series editors Martin Windrow & Nick Reynolds

OSPREY PUBLISHING
Bloomsbury Publishing Plc
Kemp House, Chawley Park, Cumnor Hill, Oxford OX2 9PH, UK
29 Earlsfort Terrace, Dublin 2, Ireland
1385 Broadway, 5th Floor, New York, NY 10018, USA
E-mail: info@ospreypublishing.com
www.ospreypublishing.com

OSPREY is a trademark of Osprey Publishing Ltd

First published in Great Britain in 2022

© Osprey Publishing Ltd, 2022

A catalogue record for this book is available from the British Library

ISBN: PB: 9781472851338; eBook: 9781472851307; ePDF: 9781472851321;
XML: 9781472851314

22 23 24 25 26 10 9 8 7 6 5 4 3 2 1

Editor: Martin Windrow
Index by Alan Rutter
Typeset by PDQ Digital Media Solutions, Bungay, UK
Printed in India by Replika Press Private Ltd.

FSC
www.fsc.org

MIX
Paper from
responsible sources
FSC® C016779

Osprey Publishing supports the Woodland Trust, the UK's leading woodland conservation charity.

To find out more about our authors and books, visit **www.ospreypublishing.com**. Here you will find extracts, author interviews, details of forthcoming events, and the option to sign up for our newsletter.

Dedication

To my parents Maria Rosaria and Benedetto, for sharing with me a life-long passion for history, and for their precious advice, which is always fundamental for me.

Acknowledgements

I am grateful to the veteran military historian Ian Heath for his expert advice. Thanks are also due to the series editor Martin Windrow, for his valuable assistance throughout the book's preparation. Another special acknowledgement goes to Giuseppe Rava, for the magnificent colour plates: thanks to his artistic brilliance, we hope that we have recreated the atmosphere of a distant but fascinating Asian conflict.

All photographs and prints reproduced in this book are in the public domain.

TITLE PAGE PHOTO:
Japanese line infantrymen firing their single-shot, bolt-action Type 18 Murata rifles from the cover of a paddy-field dyke in dry weather. This Japanese-produced weapon was standard issue to the line infantry in 1894–95; it was effective, but its big 11mm cartridge held black-powder propellant, so firing produced thick white smoke. By the outbreak of hostilities with China, only units of the Imperial Guard Division had yet received the 8mm Type 22 magazine rifle with smokeless rounds.

OPPOSITE
A Japanese line infantryman photographed shortly before his departure for the front in 1894. Note that, for technical photographic reasons, the facing colours (yellow cap band and piping, yellow rank stripes above cuffs, scarlet-red collar and shoulder straps) hardly show up against the dark blue M1886 uniform. All contemporary Japanese prints, and the uniform plates by Rühl (1900), show solid-colour facings, as described in the plate commentaries. This soldier's field marching equipment copies German models, including the M1888 ammunition pouches; his rifle is an 11mm single-shot, bolt-action Type 18 Murata, complete with a Mauser-type bayonet.

ARMIES OF THE FIRST SINO-JAPANESE WAR 1894–95

HISTORICAL BACKGROUND

The First Sino-Japanese War of 1894–95 was a landmark in modern Asian history, since it marked the ascendancy of Imperial Japan as a great regional power, and confirmed to the world Imperial China's relative military impotence. The war saw a clash between a fully-modernized Japanese state army and navy, and disunited and partly archaic Chinese forces. Under the restored Meiji dynasty, Japan had been the first major Asian state to reorganize its military forces along 'Western' lines, since the Boshin War (1868–69) against supporters of the former Tokugawa shogunate. Following 1877, when the Meiji government crushed the last *samurai* resistance in the Satsuma Rebellion, it had rapidly built up a large conscript Imperial Japanese Army and Navy, both with modern equipment.[1]

By contrast, China under the late Qing dynasty still relied for defence on very heterogeneous and mostly outdated military forces. During and since the so-called Opium Wars (1838–42 & 1856–60), Britain and France had inflicted a series of humiliating defeats on Chinese armies. The Qing had tried to reform their forces in response, but by the end of the century they had achieved little. Several modernized contingents of Chinese troops were organized between 1850 and 1894, but these

were mostly experiments carried out locally by regional 'warlords' rather than a sustained programme by the central government in Peking (modern Beijing). In the 1890s the centrally controlled Chinese army (such as it was) remained a largely archaic force, making little use of modern firearms and having a patchy grasp of up-to-date tactics.

At sea, however, the situation was different, since Chinese attempts at modernization had already achieved some positive results by 1890. Again, unlike the Japanese, the Chinese did not have a single state naval force but four autonomous (and rivalrous) regional navies. In 1884–85 one of these commands, the *Beiyang* ('Northern Seas') Fleet, deliberately avoided battle during the Tonkin War against France. Subsequently its regional authorities ordered new warships from German and British shipyards, and employed foreign instructors to train their crews. By 1894, considerable financial investments and energetic foreign officers had made the Beiyang Fleet the largest of China's navies, with a respectable operational potential.

---

1   See MAA 530, *Japanese Armies 1868–1877: The Boshin War and Satsuma Rebellion.*

An official portrait of Mutsuhito, the Meiji Emperor (b. 1852, r. 1867–1912), one of the most important figures in Japan's political history. The young monarch reformed his country following the bloody civil conflict known as the Boshin War (1868–69), against followers of the Tokugawa *shogun*, and subsequently crushed the Satsuma Rebellion (1877), the last great revolt of the *samurai* feudal warrior caste. After its victories in the First Sino-Japanese War the Meiji government increased its influence in China by intervening in the Boxer Rebellion (1900), and officially annexed Korea in 1910.

The various regional navies all included a certain number of foot troops, since they mostly operated on rivers and thus needed auxiliary landing forces. However, only the modernized Beiyang Fleet had an organized corps of naval infantry; each of its major warships had a detachment of naval infantrymen with modern firearms. The perceived threat of the Beiyang Fleet was one of the causes behind the outbreak of the First Sino-Japanese War, since the Japanese were determined to establish naval dominance in East Asia.

As it became an industrialized and (in a limited, technical sense) a 'Westernized' state, Japan began to pursue an aggressive foreign policy comparable to those of the colonial powers. The country needed large supplies of primary natural resources for its growing industry, and was determined to acquire a wider sphere of influence in East Asia. The Chinese Empire – both crumbling under the pressure exerted by the Western powers, and ravaged by civil wars – was an obvious target for Japan's expansionist ambitions.

The war of 1894–95 would be fought initially for possession of Korea, a country that had been a cause of contention between the two empires since medieval times, and which was now attracting attention from a third. The location of this strategic peninsula made it a sort of bridge between mainland Asia and the Japanese islands, and it possessed important natural resources. After a vain Japanese attempt to conquer it in 1592–98, Japan's long period of isolation under the Tokugawa shogunate had allowed the Chinese Empire to retain control of Korea without major challenges.

The opening of Korea

In 1894 Korea, although nominally an independent kingdom ruled by King Gojong of the ancient Joeson (Choson) dynasty, was in fact a tributary Chinese protectorate. Since Japan's opening to the outside world began in the 1860s, Korea's ruling elites had continued to shun modern foreign ideas as dangerously alien; meanwhile, the overseas powers wanted to open Korea, like Japan, to international trade. The first Westerners to arrive were the Americans, who sent five warships to Korea in 1871 with the aim of supporting a US diplomatic delegation. The pretext was the destruction by the Koreans in 1866 of an American merchant ship, the *General Sherman*, which had been attempting to trade along the Taedong river. The Koreans greeted the 1871 expedition with fire from their coastal batteries around Ganghwa island. Following the principles of 'gunboat diplomacy', the US Navy responded by bombarding these positions and landing a force which captured them. The Korean authorities nevertheless refused to negotiate; the squadron had to withdraw, and for a time this episode simply hardened Korea's isolationist policy.

However, by 1876 elements at the Korean royal court had become impressed by Japan's rapid modernization, and sent observers to learn more. The subsequent opening of Korea's ports to Japanese trade under the Treaty of Ganghwa began an important period of renewed Japanese influence in Korea. Initially, underestimating the impact of the Meiji reforms, the Qing Imperial government to which Korea owed fealty did not perceive this as a serious threat. However, in 1882 the Korean monarchy, already beginning its own process of modernization, signed a Treaty of Commerce and Navigation with the USA which opened the country to Western trade. This was followed by similar treaties with Great Britain and Germany (1883), Italy and Russia (1884), and France (1886).

The years following the opening of Korea also saw a growing Imperial Russian interest in the Far East, since in 1891 the construction of the Trans-Siberian Railway began. Its final completion in 1916 would connect Moscow with the port of Vladivostok, located nearly 6,000 miles away on the Pacific in the Sea of Japan, not far from the border between northern Korea and Chinese Manchuria. Long before this, its construction had already led to massive migration from European Russia into Siberia, and the transformation of its economy. Both China and Japan perceived the Russians as a potential menace to their interests.

The 'Imo incident', 1882

In January 1881 the Korean monarchy had launched an ambitious programme of administrative reforms with the aim of achieving a Japanese-style modernization – including a complete reorganization of its military forces. Since this process could only increase Japan's influence over the peninsula, China tried to hamper it as much as possible. Consequently, Korea found itself attracting the rival attentions of three great empires, while its society was being divided by animosities between traditionalists and enthusiasts for reform.

This unrest exploded in 1882, when Korea experienced a severe drought that led to food shortages and left the government on the verge of bankruptcy. Echoing a similar uprising in Japan just five years before, the traditional feudal *yangban* class – who faced loss of power due to the ongoing reforms – exploited the discontents of unpaid soldiers and hungry peasants to spark a conservative revolt against the royal government in Seoul. On 23 July 1882 much of the Korean army mutinied, and in Seoul the poor rose up in a short but bloody rebellion. During this so-called 'Imo incident' rioters attacked the Japanese legation in Seoul and killed, among others, the leader of the Japanese military mission; they also penetrated the royal palace, killing several government officials of the reformist party and forcing the queen to flee for her life. Convinced that Japan would send troops to Korea to take revenge for its murdered diplomats, the Chinese government rapidly ordered a force of 4,500 soldiers into Korea, and this soon quelled the rebellion. Japan did indeed send four warships, and a battalion to Seoul, but these arrived only after order had already been restored.

These events proved to be a major setback for Korea's modernizers. China curtailed the country's previous level of autonomy, re-asserting

Zaitian, the Guangxu Emperor (b. 1871, r. 1875–1908), the tenth monarch of the Qing dynasty, ruled China under the strong influence of his aunt, the dominant Empress Dowager Cixi (1835–1908), during most of his reign. The emperor was partly free from her control only during the decade 1889–98, when she ostensibly retired. Even then, however, Cixi continued to receive duplicates of the government's reports to the emperor, and she was still consulted regularly by senior officials.

Contemporary engraving showing the departure of Japanese troops for Korea in 1894. The infantrymen are all dressed in their M1886 dark blue uniforms, but wear the peaked (visored) service cap in the white version issued for summer use. The European figure (centre) is probably a press correspondent. (ASKB)

political control over it as a vassal state, and giving Chinese merchants privileged status in its economic affairs. Henceforth Japan's military presence would be limited to a small guard stationed in Seoul to protect their legation. During the following years two competing factions emerged within the Korean elites: conservatives, who were favourable to China's influence and hostile to further reforms, and modernizers, who looked to Japan for support.

The 'Gapsin' coup and its aftermath, 1884–86

On 4 December 1884 the modernizers of the 'Enlightenment Party' tried to seize power, hoping to take advantage of a reduction in the Chinese garrison due to China's Tonkin War with France. These reformers (with the encouragement of the Japanese ambassador, who promised the support of his legation guards) staged a coup in Seoul and proclaimed a new government. However, in a matter of days this 'Gapsin' coup was suppressed by Gen Yuan Shikai's Chinese garrison. The Qing Empire's repression was harsh: the Japanese legation was burned down, some 40 Japanese were killed, and the surviving leaders of the Korean modernizers were forced to flee into exile in Japan.

The following month, in January 1885, the Japanese responded to these events by sending seven warships and two battalions to Korea. At that time China was in no military condition to fight a full-scale war against Japan; ongoing negotiations with France would lead in another three months to a formal concession of defeat in Tonkin. The Qing government felt obliged to come to terms with Japan; a Japanese military presence in Seoul would be restored, but otherwise both China and Japan agreed to withdraw their forces from Korea. However, Gen Yuan Shikai remained in Seoul as Chinese minister in Korea, overseeing its client relationship with Beijing.

During 1885 tension between China and Japan continued to grow, not least because the Tokyo government started to show a renewed interest in the island of Formosa (modern Taiwan). This outpost of the Qing Empire had a Chinese garrison and a sizeable mercantile settler population, but in practice these had little influence over the aboriginal communities which inhabited most of the island. Japan had sent a military expedition to Formosa in 1874, in retaliation for the killing by aborigines of some shipwrecked Japanese sailors three years before. Despite the failure of a French landing force in the north to make any progress in 1884–85, Japan still harboured ambitions for Formosa.

In 1886, at a time of high tension, four modern Chinese warships of the Beiyang Fleet entered Nagasaki harbour, ostensibly to carry out repairs but in reality to provoke Japan. Some Chinese sailors started a riot in the city, during which several Japanese policemen were killed. The

Beiyang Fleet then left Japanese waters, with no Chinese government apology for the incident.

The 'Donghak rebellion', 1894

As a result of this 'Nagasaki incident', anti-Chinese feelings in Japan increased. On 28 March 1894 one of the most important of Korea's Japanese-sponsored modernizers, Kim Okgyun, was assassinated in Shanghai, causing outrage in Tokyo. Two months later, on 1 June 1894, a new revolt known as the 'Donghak rebellion' broke out in Korea. Oppressive taxation and incompetent administration by the Chinese-backed conservative government had caused renewed discontent among the Korean peasantry, who now rose up in large numbers. On 3 June King Gojong, at the insistence of Gen Yuan Shikai, requested Chinese military help to restore order.

The Qing Empire responded by sending 2,900 soldiers into Korea, with orders to crush the revolt before the Japanese had a chance to intervene. By the middle of June the Japanese already had several warships in the ports of Chemulpo (modern Inchon) and Pusan; in addition, they had disembarked a contingent of 420 naval infantrymen, who were immediately dispatched to Seoul to protect the Japanese legation. Meanwhile, in Japan, a force of 8,000 soldiers built around the 4,000-strong 9th Infantry Brigade (and known as the Oshima Composite Bde, after its commander MajGen Oshima Yoshimasa) was soon assembled and shipped to Chemulpo. The Japanese government proposed to the Chinese that their forces suppress the rebellion jointly, but the latter refused, and King Gojong demanded the immediate withdrawal of Japanese troops from Korea.

In the event, the Chinese force was slow to get into action, while the energetic Oshima Bde had crushed the Donghak rebellion by 25 June, occupying and pacifying most of southern Korea within a few weeks. The Chinese government, surprised by this rapid operation, had no intention of fighting the Japanese expedition now that southern Korea had already fallen. However, the Japanese government was determined to extend the hostilities by attacking the Chinese in northern Korea, exploiting Chinese military weakness to conquer the peninsula once and for all.

In early July, British diplomats in China tried to mediate between the two empires, but without success. At this point the Japanese ambassador presented to King Gojong a 'plan for reforms' which, if accepted, would have transformed his realm into a vassal state of Japan. When the king rejected this proposal, on 23 July Japanese troops occupied Seoul and captured Gojong in his palace. A new administration composed of Korean 'modernizers' was installed in the Korean capital, and this client government authorized Japan to expel the Chinese military forces still stationed on its territory. In fact, the Chinese tactical command known as the Beiyang Army (Gen Ye Zhichao) was already withdrawing from northern Korea, so this escalation was needless. The Chinese government rejected the new Korean administration as illegitimate, and, two days after the occupation of Seoul, on 25 July 1894 undeclared hostilities between Japan and China broke out.

CHRONOLOGY

1894:

1 June Outbreak of Donghak rebellion against Chinese-backed government of Korea.

3 June King Gojong of Korea requests Chinese military help to suppress rebellion, since his army is unreliable.

June 2,900 Chinese troops sent to north Korea; meanwhile, 8,000-strong Japanese force (MajGen Oshima) starts landing at Chemulpo (Inchon, south Korea) on **12th.** This defeats the rebels, and by the **25th** south Korea is under Japanese control.

July King Gojong rejects Japanese political proposal to accept protectorate status.

23–25 July Japanese forces in Korea replace pro-China government with new client administration, which authorizes expulsion of Chinese forces. Japanese troops occupy Seoul, and capture King Gojong.

25 July: Naval battle of Pungdo. Chinese reinforce positions at Asan Bay by sea, but Japanese cruisers intercept part of Beiyang Fleet convoy. Chinese lose 2 gunboats, suffer heavy damage to a cruiser, and a troop transport is sunk with heavy loss of life.

28 July: Battle of Seonghwan. 3,500 isolated Chinese troops, entrenched without artillery on Ansong river inland from Asan Bay, are heavily defeated by 4,000 Japanese under MajGen Oshima.

31 July: Qing Empire declares war on Japan; official outbreak of First Sino-Japanese War.

1 September Corps-strength tactical Japanese First Army (Gen Yamagata Aritomo) created.

15 September: Battle of Pyongyang. After some 12 hours' fighting, Gen Ye Zhichau's 13,000-plus Chinese troops surrender north Korea's main city to 18,000 attackers from Japanese First Army (5th Div, part 3rd Div) under LtGen Nozu Michitsura. Survivors flee north to Yalu river border between Korea and Chinese Manchuria, leaving Japanese in control of entire Korean territory.

17 September: Naval battle of Yalu River. Off mouth of river, following Chinese troop landings, Japanese Combined Fleet (Adm Sukeyuki Ito) defeats Chinese Beiyang Fleet (Adm Ting Juchang) in decisive naval action of the war; 6 IJN warships damaged, 5 Chinese cruisers sunk.

27 September Japanese Second Army created (Gen Oyama Iwao).

24 October Japanese invasion of Manchuria begins. Chinese defenders of line on north bank of Yalu, centred on Juliencheng, are overstretched; some 13,000 troops of Japanese First Army bridge river, and break through with ease at two points. On same day, Japanese Second Army begins landings at Pitzuwo on east coast of Liaodong Peninsula.

25–30 October Japanese First Army divides into two commands. 3rd Div (LtGen Katsura Taro) heads north-west across base of Liaodong Peninsula to prevent its reinforcement, while 5th Div-plus (Gen Oku Yasukata) advances north to threaten Liaoyang and Mukden (modern Shenyang).

3–10 November Japanese Second Army advances south towards Lushun (Port Arthur), and captures outlying positions at Jinzhou and Talien, from which Chinese survivors retreat to Port Arthur.

21 November: Capture of Port Arthur. Garrison surrenders after only hours of fighting. Thereafter large (but unconfirmed) numbers of Chinese prisoners and civilians are killed in so-called 'Port Arthur massacre'.

28–29 November Anti-Japanese Korean Peasant Army defeated at Chongju, Korea.

13 December First Army occupies Haicheng, Manchuria.

1895:

10 January Second Army captures Kaiping (modern Gaizhou) in north-west of Liaodong Peninsula.

18 January Japanese Navy bombards Chefoo (Dengzhou) on Shandong Peninsula; Second Army begins landing at Yungcheng, east of Weihaiwei harbour (modern Weihai), base of surviving Beiyang Fleet.

30 January–2 February Second Army takes Weihaiwei in three days' fighting.

1–10 February Japanese Navy attacks trapped Beiyang Fleet; all Chinese torpedo boats are sunk or captured. Adml Ting's flagship, battleship *Dingyuan*, is scuttled to prevent its capture, and Adml Ting commits suicide; thereafter remaining warships of Beiyang Fleet surrender.

16 February In Manchuria, repulse of fifth Chinese attack on First Army troops holding Haicheng.

28 February–4 March Japanese First Army offensive against Niuzhuang and Liaoyang. **3 March**, bulk of 3rd Div invests Liaoyang; **4 March**, Niuzhuang occupied by 5th and part-3rd Div after hard street fighting.

March Gen Nozu replaces Gen Yamagata in command of Japanese First Army. Chinese-Japanese peace negotiations begin on **20th.**

23–26 March Japanese occupy Pescadores Islands, between mainland China and Formosa (modern Taiwan).

24 March Japanese landing force takes Haichow (Lianyungang), south of Shandong Peninsula.

17 April: Treaty of Shimonoseki ends First Sino-Japanese War. Korea becomes Japanese vassal state, and China also cedes to Japan the Pescadores Islands, Formosa, and much of Liaodong Peninsula (though the latter will soon be returned to China, under European pressure).

23 May Refusing terms of Treaty of Shimonoseki, Chinese authorities in Formosa declare independent Republic.

30 May–14 June Japanese Imperial Guard Div lands near Keelung. Republican government flees by **6th**, and by **14th** Japanese have occupied northern Formosa.

15 June–21 October Despite stubborn resistance from Formosan guerrillas and Gen Liu Yongfu's Chinese 'Black Flag' mercenaries, Imperial Guard Div gradually advances down western half of island to secure central and southern Formosa. **27/28 August**, Japanese victory in night battle at Baguashan, near Changhwa, opens way into south. Although delayed by disease and difficult logistics, reinforced Japanese advance culminates in occupation of Tainan on **21 October**, effectively ending campaign.

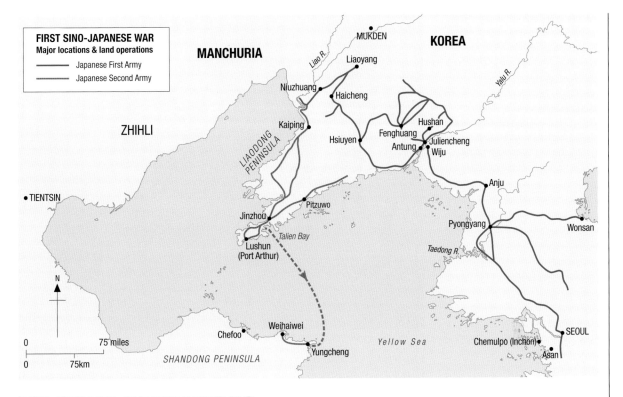

MILITARY OPERATIONS

By the end of July 1894 the Chinese forces in Korea, about 3,500 strong, were in a difficult situation: they could be supplied only by sea through Asan Bay, about 30 miles south-west of Japanese-occupied Seoul. However, to organize an effective naval blockade of Asan, and to assure their own future transport and supply of major land forces in Korea, the Japanese navy would have to neutralize the Qing warships of the Beiyang Fleet, which had already moved into the Yellow Sea. At this time each fleet had 12 medium and heavy warships, but they varied in their additional light units.

In 1894 the Imperial Japanese Navy was still strongly influenced by the British Royal Navy, but the withdrawal of British instructors in 1879 had led in the early 1880s to the adoption of a new French tactical doctrine. This favoured the use of lighter, faster (and cheaper) cruisers and small torpedo boats over that of heavier capital ships. In summer 1894 the IJN comprised the following units: 8 'protected' cruisers (i.e. armoured on the decks only) – 3 British-built, 2 French-built and 3 built in Japan; 1 British-built cruiser; 1 British-built 'ironclad' battleship; 2 British-built armoured corvettes; 26 torpedo boats; plus several auxiliary armed merchant cruisers and converted passenger ships. Following mobilization, these units were assembled into a single division of warships and three flotillas of torpedo boats.

The Chinese Beiyang Fleet's strength was based on 2 German-built ironclad battleships, the *Dingyuan* and *Zhenyuan*. The fleet also had 2 excellent German-built armoured cruisers, *Laiyuan* and *Jingyuan*; 2 British-built protected cruisers; 4 torpedo cruisers; 1 coastal battleship and 1 corvette, both Chinese-built; 13 torpedo boats and several river

gunboats, plus auxiliary chartered merchant steamers. Thus each fleet had 12 main units, but the IJN had an advantage in torpedo boats of 26 to 13; it also enjoyed more fundamental advantages (see below, 'Naval battle of the Yalu river').

Naval battle of Pungdo, 25 July 1894

Given the need to deploy and supply its troops overseas, Japan's strategic approach to the war would inevitably be shaped by the outcome of an early naval confrontation.

Soon after the outbreak of hostilities, the Japanese detached a 'flying squadron' of three protected cruisers commanded by Rear Adm Tsuboi Kozo to Chemulpo (Inchon) on Korea's west coast. A planned rendezvous there with another Japanese cruiser and a gunboat failed to take place, and the Chinese successfully landed reinforcements further south at Asan Bay from two of three chartered British steamers escorted by a cruiser and two gunboats. After putting back to sea two of these escorts were pursued by the IJN flying squadron, which drove the Chinese gunboat *Kwangyi* aground and seriously damaged the cruiser *Jiyuan*. While in close pursuit of *Jiyuan*, the Japanese cruisers encountered the third Chinese transport, *Gaosheng*, still heading for Asan Bay escorted by the gunboat *Tsaokiang*. When the latter fled westwards with the *Jiyuan*, Adml Tsuboi divided his squadron: two cruisers pursued the *Jiyuan* and the gunboat, while the *Naniwa* headed for the troopship. In what became known as the battle of Pungdo, the *Jiyuan* took further damage, but once again escaped; the gunboat surrendered; and the *Gaosheng* was sunk, taking to the bottom some 800 Chinese troops and 12 guns.

The Beiyang Fleet did make two further sorties into the Yellow Sea from Weihaiwei on the Shandong Peninsula during July and August, but did not encounter the IJN. (Naval manoeuvres throughout the war were hampered by the fact that forces could only locate one another by the sight of smoke above the horizon.)

Battle of Seonghwan, 28 July 1894

Thus deprived of some reinforcements and artillery, the isolated Chinese troops who were entrenched on part of the Ansong river, north-east from Asan Bay, were attacked by 4,000 Japanese under MajGen Oshima. Although not greatly outnumbered, the Chinese were heavily defeated, and only small numbers managed to escape northwards to Pyongyang. The Japanese then occupied Asan, assuming complete control over central Korea. (It should be noted that the battles of Pungdo and Seongwhan preceded the Qing Empire's formal declaration of war on Japan, which followed on 31 July.)

Battle of Pyongyang, 15 September 1894

Chinese forces under Gen Ye Zhichau enjoyed strong positions in Pyongyang, since the city was protected on the south and east by the navigable Taedong river, and was dominated from the north by Chinese-held hills. In total, the Qing government had assembled at least 13,000 soldiers in this main city of northern Korea: 8,000 were sent by sea, 5,000 made a difficult overland march southwards through Manchuria, and additional modest numbers of survivors had arrived from Asan. The Chinese had 4 field artillery pieces, 28 mountain guns and 6 machine guns, but were short of artillery ammunition. The garrison were ordered to build major earthwork defences on the south-west front, which was the most open approach for attackers.

The initial 8,000 Japanese soldiers of MajGen Oshima's reinforced brigade had by now been joined by 10,000 troops of the new corps-sized Japanese First Army (Gen Yamagata Aritomo). This consisted of the 3rd and 5th Divisions, which had begun landing at Chemulpo on 12 June. During August–September they marched north towards Pyongyang, linking with reinforcements landed through the ports of Wonsan and Pusan on the east and south coasts. Japan's aim was to drive the Chinese out of Korea before the coming of harsh winter weather could slow their offensive.

The Japanese attacked early on 15 September, under overall command of the 5th Div's LtGen Nozu Michitsura (due to Gen Yamagata's illness). The bulk of the 5th and 3rd Divs attacked the south-west defences, and

Typically animated Japanese print depicting infantrymen of the 5th Division early on the morning of 24 October 1894, fighting their way across the pontoon bridge erected across the Yalu river opposite the Chinese positions at Juliencheng.

Oshima's Composite Bde the riverside forts to the south-east; meanwhile the detached so-called Wonsan and Sangnyong columns (led respectively by Col Sato Tadashi, 18th Inf Regt, and MajGen Tatsumi Naofumi, 10th Inf Bde) made diversionary flanking attacks on the north-east. The fighting was hardest in the south-west, where the defenders initially repulsed all assaults; late in the day heavy rain turned the new earthworks into a sea of mud, and after dark the Japanese gave up some of the ground they had gained. These units were unaware that the flanking columns had made unexpected progress, capturing the Chinese fortress of Moktan-tei on the hills north of Pyongyang, and thus gaining dominating positions for Japanese artillery to bombard the defenders from the rear. The Chinese surrendered or fled northwards, and when the Japanese main force renewed its advance on the 16th it found the defences abandoned. The Japanese had captured Pyongyang at a reported cost of just 102 men killed and 433 wounded, against alleged Chinese casualties of some 2,000 killed and 4,000 wounded (note that all such claimed figures remain unconfirmed). It has been stated that this defeat cost the Chinese the majority of their best *Huai* Army volunteers (see below, 'Chinese Army; the *Yung-Ying* Armies'), leaving them with only ill-trained and ill-led conscripts to fight the later battles.

Following the fall of Pyongyang, the Japanese First Army could advance north to the Yalu river, which marked the border between Korea and Chinese Manchuria. Although Japan now controlled the whole of Korea, the Meiji government was determined to press on into Qing home territory.

Naval battle of the Yalu river, 17 September 1894
Even before the fall of Pyongyang the Chinese occupied strong defences on the Yalu river, though they lacked the numbers to man them strongly. On 16 September the Beiyang Fleet (Adm Ting Juchang) arrived off the mouth of the Yalu, where the main force anchored in a defensive deployment, while the coastal battleship and three torpedo and gunboats escorted transports about 12 miles up-river to land some 4,500 reinforcements. At mid-morning on 17 September the escorts were still returning to the river mouth when Japanese warships were sighted on the horizon.

Admiral Ito Sukeyuki's Combined Fleet consisted of his own Main Fleet, with 2 ironclads, 4 cruisers and a gunboat, and Adm Tsuboi's

Flying Squadron with 4 cruisers. The Beiyang Fleet was deployed with the battleships *Dingyuan* and *Zhenyuan* in the centre, flanked by two wings: on the left were 2 cruisers and a corvette (the latter provided, reluctantly, by the Guangdong Fleet), and on the right the best armoured cruisers *Laiyuan* and *Jingyuan* and 3 other cruisers. In reserve were the returning escort from the landing operation: the coastal battleship *Pingyan*, a torpedo boat and 2 gunboats. Admiral Ting tried to form a single battle-line across the mouth of the Yalu, but failures of communication resulted in a wedge-shaped deployment echeloned backwards from the two battleships. While the Chinese had a slight advantage in numbers, this was off-set by the IJN's superior quality. The Japanese ships were mostly faster, and were better maintained; most mounted faster-firing guns, with superior range and arcs of fire; their crews were better trained, especially in gunnery, and had more – and more reliable – ammunition.

The Japanese approached from the west in column, led by Adm Tsuboi's squadron. When ordered to attack the Chinese right wing, Tsuboi slashed across the enemy fleet's front, holding his fire while the Chinese wasted ammunition by firing when still out of range. He then rounded their right flank, badly damaging 2 cruisers, before heading up-river to engage the returning escort flotilla. When he turned south again, he fired upon the enemy line while the IJN Main Fleet engaged it from its left flank. Together Ito's and Tsuboi's units broke up, encircled and hammered the Beiyang Fleet. While they failed to penetrate the heaviest armour, their quicker-firing guns decimated deck crews and smashed superstructures (including the bridge of Adm Ting's flagship, *Matsushima*). Although at short range the Chinese heavy guns did considerable damage to 4 of the IJN vessels and some to 2 others, the Japanese lost no ships, while 4 Chinese cruisers were sunk and another scuttled. The survivors limped away to their repair facilities at Lushun (Port Arthur) at the tip of the Liaodong Peninsula.

Johann Schönberg, himself a veteran of the Austrian army in 1866, covered wars in four continents over nearly 40 years, between the American Civil War in the 1860s and the Boxer Rebellion in 1900. He worked his paintings up from drawings and watercolours made on the spot – here, while accompanying the Japanese First Army on the march in snow-bound Manchuria early in 1895. The soldiers all wear their dark blue greatcoats, to which hoods have been added – probably made at unit level? (ASKB)

Japanese invasion of Manchuria, October–November 1894

The Chinese land forces, now numbering some 23,000 under Gen Song Qin, remained on the defensive in their Yalu line, protected by entrenchments and redoubts over some 20 miles, roughly from Antung (modern Dandong) in the south to Hushan in the north, and centred on the walled city of Juliencheng (Chiulien). The Japanese First Army initially fielded only some 10,000 men, but received 3,000 reinforcements on 10 October.

On 24 October, the Japanese opened a new front by beginning to land their Second Army (Gen Oyama Iwao) at Pitsuwo (modern Pikou), about 60 miles north of Port Arthur on the east coast of the Liaodong Peninsula; and that night Gen Yamagata launched First Army's offensive against the Yalu line. His engineers had already made preparations,

Impression of Japanese Second Army infantrymen storming one of the Chinese defensive positions around Lushun (Port Arthur) in November 1894; the anchorage in the left background suggests that this represents a battery above Talien Bay. Two field guns have been emplaced beside the heavy fortress carriages of what seem to be 15cm Krupp guns, typical of China's German and British imports. The Japanese would eventually report the capture of 220 such heavy weapons in the Lushun defensive complex.

and that night a pontoon bridge was completed opposite Juliencheng, apparently without being detected. The successful attack across this by 5th Div was in fact a secondary effort, while 3rd Div outflanked the defences at Hushan the following day. Neither assault was resisted for more than a matter of hours. On 26 October Antung was also taken, along with much abandoned equipment and stores.

While Gen Song Qin fell back northwards towards Liaoyang, two separate commands of Japanese First Army advanced. While 5th Div (now commanded by Gen Oku Yasukata) pushed north to threaten Liaoyang and beyond it Mukden (modern Shenyang), on its left 3rd Div (Gen Katsura) cut north-westwards across the base of the Liaodong Peninsula, occupying Fenghuang (modern Fengcheng) and Hsiuyen (modern Xiuyan) on 30 October and 15 November respectively.

Liaodong Peninsula: capture of Port Arthur, 21 November 1894

Meanwhile, on the Liaodong Peninsula, the Second Army (1st and 2nd Divs, 12th Composite Bde from 6th Div) was meeting only negligible resistance as it marched south. Its objective was the modern French-built naval base of Lushun (Port Arthur), where the mauled Beiyang Fleet was under repair. China's only harbour offering this capability, Lushun was only about 150 miles due east from Tientsin near the coast of Zhihli province, and thus controlled the sea approaches to the capital, Beijing. In keeping with its importance, it was protected by surrounding hill forts and defended by heavy Krupp and Armstrong artillery. The size of Gen Wei Rugui's garrison in the whole complex has been estimated at perhaps 10,000, but this is unconfirmed.

On 3 November, MajGen Nogi Maresuke left Pitzuwo with his 1st Inf Bde, the vanguard of 1st Div (Gen Yamaji Motoharu). After minor skirmishing the following day, on the 5th–6th the Second Army's first serious engagement led to the capture of the walled town of Jinzhou guarding the narrowest part of the promontory. On 7 November the Japanese took the forts defending the naval anchorage at Talien (modern Dalian) Bay; in all these engagements the defenders fired furiously but unskilfully on the assault troops, and soon fled once the infantry met in combat. The Qing government had ordered the surviving units of the Beiyang Fleet to sail 80 miles south to Weihaiwei (modern Weihai) on the Shandong Peninsula, from where it could still theoretically protect the sea approaches to Beijing. However, the fleet was further weakened when the battleship *Zhenyuan* ran aground on rocks outside that port, where it remained out of commission for the rest of the war.

It cost Gen Oyama time and difficulty to bring up his siege train of 36 guns, and it was 20 November before soldiers of the Second Army began skirmishing with the defenders of Port Arthur itself. This created panic among the Chinese troops, and led to riots among the city's inhabitants. Before dawn on 21 November the Japanese stormed the city, led by 1st Div; Gen Yamaji had expected stubborn resistance and heavy casualties, but in the event the Chinese repeated their behaviour in the outlying forts, and the entire garrison surrendered soon after mid-day. (For his failure, Gen Wei Rugui would be executed by the Qing government in January 1895.)

Some accounts claim that isolated parties of Chinese troops fired upon the Japanese entering after the surrender; others, that the attackers were incensed to find the bodies of their casualties mutilated. Whatever the truth, over the next two to three days Japanese soldiers killed perhaps hundreds, perhaps thousands of prisoners and civilians, in what became known as the 'Port Arthur massacre'.

Shandong Peninsula: battle of Weihaiwei, 18 January–10 February 1895

The Japanese were still determined to destroy what remained of the Beiyang Fleet. This consisted of three warships and 13 torpedo boats, which were at anchor in Weihaiwei harbour on the Shandong Peninsula, protected by booms and by 12 forts with modern artillery. On 18 January the IJN began a bombardment of Chefoo (Dengzhou – modern Yantai) about 30 miles west of Weihaiwei. This was a diversion from landings by Second Army (2nd Div, part 6th Div) at Yungcheng east of Weihaiwai, which lasted from 18 to 22 January. The landing force advanced on the 26th, by both a coast road and an inland route, reaching Weihaiwei on 29 January. A three-pronged assault began the following day; although hampered by snow, and initially strong opposition, the Japanese entered the city on 2 February. By this time most of the garrison had withdrawn, and the Japanese captured 36 emplaced guns and many field pieces. (Major-General Odera Yasuzumi of 12th Inf Bde, killed by shellfire, was the only Japanese general officer to die in combat during the war.)

With the coastal batteries in Japanese hands, the IJN was able to make torpedo-boat attacks on the trapped Chinese fleet, culminating in a general attack on 7 February. Several Chinese torpedo-boats attempted to escape, but all were destroyed or captured. On 10 February, Adml Ting Ruchang scuttled his flagship *Dingyuan* and committed suicide, and the remaining warships surrendered.

Manchuria: battle of Niuzhuang, 28 February 1895

On 13 December 1894, Japanese First Army had occupied the walled city of Haicheng on their Manchurian front, and on 10 January 1895, Second Army elements had captured Kaiping (modern Gaizhou) about 32 miles

大寺将軍弾丸為ニ斃繋百尺崖之圖

Print of a Japanese Second Army officer and soldiers in a captured battery (again, accompanied by a Western war correspondent), watching an IJN attack on the trapped Beiyang Fleet in Weihaiwei harbour on the Shandong Peninsula. These actions took place in early February 1895; note the falling snow visible against the dark uniforms and guns.

south-west of Haicheng on the Liaodong Peninsula. During December–January the Qing forces achieved a certain numerical advantage in Manchuria, assembling approximately 40,000 troops. About half of these were around Niuzhuang, a few miles north-west of Haicheng, and half at Liaoyang, about 60 miles away to the north-east and 40 miles south of Mukden. The Japanese needed to remove these obstacles to their front and right flanks before potentially hooking westwards and southwards to threaten Beijing itself.

On 16 February, Gen Li Kunyi committed 16,000 Chinese troops to a fifth attempt to recapture Haicheng, but they were again repulsed. Now news of the fall of Weihaiwei reached Manchuria, and Chinese desertions increased. On 28 February the Japanese launched an offensive against both Niuzhuang and Liaoyang; Chinese troops were driven back in disorderly retreat upon these two cities, and the former was occupied by the Japanese after hard street fighting. The First Army invested Liaoyang while its western operations continued for several more days, with the capture or bombardment of coastal forts.

By the beginning of March 1895, however, it became clear that the Qing Empire was on the verge of military collapse, and the Meiji government chose to increase its diplomatic pressure by organizing an amphibious landing at Haichow, south of the Shandong Peninsula and north of Shanghai, on 24 March. The Japanese capture of Haichow's fortifications was the last combat action of the war in mainland China; it put Japanese troops within 50 miles of a strategic waterway leading to Beijing, and the Qing court had no choice but to negotiate surrender.

Treaty of Shimonoseki, and occupation of Pescadores, 20 March–17 April 1895

The peace talks between China and Japan began on 20 March 1895, and ended on 17 April with the signature of the Treaty of Shimonoseki. Under its terms, the Qing Empire renounced suzerainty over the Kingdom of Korea, which was to become a Japanese vassal state. China also agreed to cede to Japan the Pescadores Islands, lying between the mainland and Formosa (modern Taiwan); Formosa itself; and the eastern portion of the Liaodong Peninsula (though this latter concession was soon renounced under pressure from the Western powers). China also had to pay Japan enormous war reparations, and grant its merchants favoured status in international trade.

Formally, the war was over; but Japan still had to occupy its territorial prizes. A month before the treaty was concluded, on 15 March the Meiji government had already assembled a 5,500-man expeditionary force for the Pescadores Islands. This archipelago was garrisoned by 5,000 Chinese troops, and its coastal defences had recently been reinforced, but the Japanese landings met very little resistance. The Chinese garrison surrendered after their coastal fortifications were shelled; the Japanese were able to occupy the islands in three days (23–26 March), although they subsequently lost some 1,500 men to disease there.

Japanese occupation of Formosa, 29 May–21 October 1895

When news of the Treaty of Shimonoseki reached Formosa, on 23 May the Chinese elite in the capital, Taipei, proclaimed – to the fury of the Beijing government – the establishment of a republic independent of both China and Japan. The Qing governor Tang Jingsong became the first president, backed by Gen Chiu Fengjia, who commanded a numerous *Hakka* Chinese militia. The Chinese Gen Liu Yongfu (the redoubtable veteran leader of 'Black Flag' mercenaries in the Tonkin War against France) was invited out of retirement to serve as overall commander of the new Formosan army, with his headquarters at Tainan in the south. Meanwhile, Japan assembled a 7,000-strong expeditionary corps around the Imperial Guard Division (Gen Prince Kitashirakawa Yoshinisa), which had not yet seen action in the war.

On 29 May the Japanese transports reached the northern coast of Formosa, and landings near Keelung proceeded over the next few days.

Part of a print representing infantrymen of the Imperial Guard Div in action on Formosa in summer 1895; they wear blue winter service caps with their white uniforms, while their officers (as always in this series of prints) retain the blue winter patrol jacket; all wear their greatcoats slung in a 'horseshoe roll'. The thick smoke generated by their black-powder ammunition is realistically depicted.

The Japanese advanced inland, initially meeting some resistance; however, by 6 June the republic's government had abandoned the island (though not Gen Liu Yongfu, who assumed the presidency). The unpaid and now leaderless Chinese garrison in the north began deserting, and looted Taipei and Tamsui. Alarmed, the leading local merchants appealed to the Japanese to restore order; the Imperial Guards entered both cities on 7 June, and quickly crushed the rioters. By 14 June the northern part of the island was under Japanese control, and most of the captured Chinese soldiers had already been repatriated. The Japanese authorities believed that occupying central and southern Formosa would present little more difficulty, but their lack of local intelligence deceived them.

Beyond the north, the Qing Empire had never exercised direct control over the hinterland of Formosa. The rest of the fever-ridden island was inhabited by independent and warlike aboriginal communities, who were masters of the heavily wooded terrain, and, although they lacked modern firearms, were expert guerrilla fighters. The main Japanese objective was Tainan, where Gen Liu now had 8 battalions of his old Black Flags. Scattered guerrilla activity slowed the Japanese advance down the west side of the island for three to four months, during which repeated ambushes provoked brutal reprisals. The defenders' disunity and Japanese tactical skill allowed the Imperial Guard Div to win a significant night battle over some 5,000 rebels supported by an artillery battery at Baguashan on 27–28 August, opening the way into the south. Suffering heavy losses to disease, and with uncertain logistics,

Detail from a group photo of Japanese officers during the war, many of them displaying gold staff aiguillettes from the right shoulder. Nearly all of them wear the dark blue 'patrol jacket' service tunic, with black silk frogging and 'Hungarian knots' on the sleeves identifying their ranks (compare with Plate A2). In the front row, at right and extreme left, are two men wearing civilian clothing but with coloured chrysanthemum badges on their left sleeve; presumably these are Imperial functionaries of some sort?

the expeditionary division received substantial reinforcements from LtGen Nogi Maresuke's 2nd Inf Div landed in the south. They reached Tainan early in October, and a three-pronged assault forced Gen Liu to surrender on 12 October. Tainan was occupied nine days later, and organized resistance ceased soon afterwards. Japanese reports list their casualties as 164 killed and 515 wounded, but at least 3,000 also died of disease (including Prince Kitashirakawa).

JAPANESE ARMY

Conscription

In January 1873, with the help of a French military mission, the Meiji government first established a system of seven years' military conscription among able-bodied males aged 20–40. The terms were modified in 1879 and again in 1883, with Prussian influence replacing that of the French, and by the eve of the First Sino-Japanese War the period of army service was 15 years starting at the age of 17. For the first three years conscripts, drawn by lot from among their year group each January, served in a '3rd Reserve' militia (*Kokumingun*). For the next three years all conscripts served in the Active Army (*Jobigun*); they then passed for four years into the 1st Reserve (*Yobigun*), which involved annual training periods, and was mostly used to augment active units from peacetime to wartime establishment and to form depots. Finally, they spent five years in the 2nd Reserve (*Kobigun*). This category had originally been liable for call-up only in national emergencies; now it included the men exempted by lottery from regular service (who had formerly formed the 3rd Reserve), and had to provide garrison troops in time of war. Non-commissioned officers did not pass into the Reserves, but spent their whole service in the Active Army.

Since 1883 most previous exemptions had been withdrawn, but the great majority of the rank-and-file still came from the poorest peasant families, since the sons of the wealthy and educated classes still found ways to avoid compulsory military service. Most of the initial officer class in the new professional army had been former *samurai* of the hereditary warrior caste, who had fought in the Boshin War and against the Satsuma Rebellion. With the passage of years these men came to embrace Western technology and doctrine, and individuals who showed unswerving loyalty to the emperor rose to the highest ranks.

Formations and strength

In 1888, under Prussian influence, the original 1873 structure of six military districts was reorganized as six territorial divisions (Tokyo, Sendai, Nagoya, Osaka, Hiroshima and Kunamoto); the northern island of Hokkaido was excluded, having only a local militia rather than raising line troops. Each division was to be fully mobile and self-sufficient, comprising units from each branch of service raised in that territory: two brigades of infantry (each of 2 regiments, each with 3 battalions); a

Details from one of ten Japanese uniform plates published by Moritz Rühl of Leipzig in 1900.

(Left) General in parade dress. Black shako with white-over-red tuft, gold lace and chrysanthemum badge; dark blue uniform, with all-gold collar, gold cord shoulder straps, 'Hungarian knots', double staff aiguillettes, buttons, and sword knot; red frontal piping; red-and-silver sash, silver tassels; red German-style ' '*Lampassen*' on trousers – two stripes flanking central piping.

(Right) Cavalry staff officer, service dress. Black undress shako with gold lace; dark blue 'Attila' jacket with black frogging and 'Hungarian knots', gold single staff aiguillettes; red trousers with green stripe flanked by pipings.

cavalry regiment (with 3 squadrons); an artillery regiment (with 4 field and 2 mountain batteries); an engineer battalion (with 3 companies); a logistic 'train' battalion (with 2 companies); and 2 companies of stretcher-bearers. Two of the six territorial divisions could be grouped together to form an 'army' (in Western terms, an army corps); thus, by 1894, Japan had the possibility of deploying three field armies.

By the outbreak of the First Sino-Japanese War the Imperial Japanese Army had a total of 67,000 regular troops; these were increased to 90,000 by the mobilization of the 1st Reserve, and then to 161,000 by mobilization of the 2nd Reserve. Another 60,000 militiamen were also called up to serve as garrison troops or to fulfill other auxiliary functions in Japan. During 1873–78 Japan had had a Marine Corps comprising infantrymen and artillerymen; after this was stood down, its landing duties began to be performed by temporary 'naval brigades' made up of sailors taken from the crews of the Imperial Japanese Navy's battleships.

Imperial Guard

In 1873 the formerly clan-based Imperial Guard *(Goshimpei)* was completely reorganized, with new conscripts drawn from every corner of Japan after a special selection. In 1888 it was redesignated the Imperial Guard Division, and began to evolve into the following structure: two brigades of infantry (each of 2 regiments, each with 2 battalions); a

Three useful views of line infantry rankers' service dress, with field marching equipment clearly modelled on German patterns, including a knapsack with an unshaven hide flap, a canvas 'breadbag' and metal canteen. With this order of dress the greatcoat is rolled and strapped to the knapsack. Once again, the period photography makes almost all coloured facings invisible, except the sleeve rank stripe of the private 1st class (centre). Note the top strap and outside buttons of the whitened canvas gaiters.

Detail from a photo of line infantrymen wearing campaign dress, with their dark blue greatcoats carried around the body *en banderole*. Although invisible here, the piping and band of the cap are yellow, the collar, shoulder straps and trouser stripe scarlet-red.

(continued on page 29)

JAPANESE IMPERIAL GUARD DIVISION
1: Sergeant 1st class, Artillery Brigade
2: Captain, 1st Infantry Regiment
3: Corporal, Cavalry Regiment

A

B

JAPANESE LINE UNITS
1: Private 1st class, 6th Inf Regt, 3rd Div, summer
2: Trooper, 5th Cav Regt, 5th Div
3: Gunner, 1st Arty Regt, 1st Div, winter

JAPANESE NAVY & GENDARMERIE
1: Seaman, landing-party, summer
2: Senior petty officer
3: Major, Gendarmerie

C

CHINA: BEIJING BANNERMEN
1: Swordsman, Tiger-Hunting Battalion
2: Rifleman, Inner units, Firearms Division
3: Guardsman, Imperial Bodyguard

D

CHINA: HEREDITARY & VOLUNTEER ARMIES
1: Manchu horse-archer, Army of the Eight Banners
2: Musketeer, Army of the Green Standard
3: Volunteer, *Huai* Army

E

CHINA: 'NEWLY CREATED ARMY' & *BEIYANG FLEET*
1: Infantry NCO, Newly-Created Army
2: Officer, *Beiyang Fleet*
3: Marine, *Beiyang Fleet*

F

KOREAN ARMY
1: Guardsman, Royal Bodyguard
2: Rifleman, Capital Guards Garrison
3: Archer, Palace Guards Garrison

DEFENDERS OF FORMOSA
1: Standard-bearer, Formosan Republican Army
2: Warrior, *Hua-hoan* tribes
3: Warrior, *Ya-hoan* tribes

cavalry regiment (with 3 squadrons); a brigade of artillery (with 4 field batteries); an engineer battalion (with 2 companies); and a train battalion (with 2 companies).

Infantry, cavalry and artillery units

The 24 infantry regiments each had 3 battalions, each with 4 companies. An infantry regiment totalled 2,320 men in peacetime and 3,280 in wartime; a battalion mustered 768 men (peacetime) and 1,088 (wartime), and a company 192 soldiers (peacetime) and 272 (wartime). A wartime company comprised a captain, 2 lieutenants, 3 second-lieutenants; a sergeant-major, a quartermaster-sergeant, 8 sergeants, 16 corporals; 8 buglers, and 232 privates. Each company could be divided into 4 platoons, and each platoon into 4 squads.

The Japanese cavalry consisted of just 6 regiments, each of 3 squadrons. Each squadron numbered 144 horsemen (peacetime) and 200 (wartime). Each squadron could be divided into 4 troops, and each troop into 4 sections.

The 6 artillery regiments each had 3 battalions, of which 2 were of field artillery and 1 was of mountain artillery. Each battalion had 2 batteries each of 6 guns, organized into three 2-gun sections. Artillery regiments were commanded by a colonel, battalions by a major, batteries by a captain, sections by a lieutenant, and individual gun crews by a sergeant. Each peacetime battery comprised 5 officers, 10 NCOs and 96 gunners; in wartime each field battery received 38 additional gunners, and each mountain battery 30.

In addition to the field and mountain battalions, the IJA also had several companies of garrison artillery, mostly tasked with manning the guns of Japan's fortified harbours. By 1894 these companies were organized into 3 regiments, each of which usually had 3 battalions of 3 or 4 companies. Peacetime garrison artillery companies comprised 5 officers, 10 NCOs and 110 gunners.

Engineer, train, and Gendarmerie units

By 1888 the IJA had 6 battalions of engineers, each of 3 companies. The battalion staff included a major, a lieutenant, a second-lieutenant, and 3 NCOs. A peacetime company had 125 men (increased to 221 in wartime), to which were attached a number of non-combatant civilian labourers. In addition to these units, each division also had a small telegraph section of 27 specialist engineers.

The Train Corps consisted of 6 battalions, each with 2 companies. Each battalion consisted of 14 officers, 42 NCOs, 540 rankers, 2 doctors, 2 veterinary-surgeons, and 12 non-combatants, and had a total of 240 horses. On wartime mobilization the train battalions were immediately broken down into small detachments that were assigned to the various field formations.

Front and rear views of Imperial Guard cavalry rankers (compare with Plate A3); the inconsistent contrasts are due to a shadow falling over the right-hand man. Note the size of the interwoven shoulder cords with trefoil knots attached to the dark blue 'Attila' jackets. The sergeant 1st class (left) has two shallow and one deep forearm stripes all matching the frogging and edging – amaranth-red. The single white stripe below them on his cuff was presented after three years' service (but was not always seen). The trooper (right) displays the elaborate decorative lace on the collar, rear seams and skirt, also in amaranth-red. Both men wear red breeches with a narrow cavalry-green sidestripe (invisible at this angle), and black hussar boots with strap-on spurs.

Japanese line artillerymen photographed on campaign; in reality, all their uniform facing details were yellow. As a gun-captain, the sergeant 1st class (left) has been issued with a small pair of binoculars. His gunners all wear two 'horseshoe rolls', one the blue greatcoat and the other apparently of pale canvas tent cloth, containing rations and small kit. Note that they are all armed with short swords, and lack any ammunition pouches.

Basic Japanese order of battle, 1894–95

FIRST ARMY: Gen Yamagata Aritomo, *later* **Gen Nozu Michitsura**

3rd Division (Nagoya): LtGen Katsura Taro
5th Infantry Brigade:
6th & 18th Infantry Regiments
6th Infantry Brigade:
7th & 19th Infantry Regiments

3rd Cavalry Regiment
3rd Artillery Regiment
3rd Engineer Battalion

5th Division (Hiroshima): LtGen Nozu Michitsura, *later* **LtGen Oku Yasukata**
9th Inf Bde:
11th & 21st Inf Regts
10th Inf Bde:
12th & 22nd Inf Regts

5th Cav Regt
5th Arty Regt
5th Eng Bn

SECOND ARMY: Gen Oyama Iwao

1st Division (Tokyo): LtGen Yamaji Motoharu
1st Inf Bde:
1st & 15th Inf Regts
2nd Inf Bde:
2nd & 3rd Inf Regts

1st Cav Regt
1st Arty Regt
1st Eng Bn

2nd Division (Sendai): LtGen Sakuma Sakata, *later* **LtGen Nogi Maresuke**
3rd Inf Bde:
4th & 16th Inf Regts
4th Inf Bde:
5th & 17th Inf Regts

2nd Cav Regt
2nd Arty Regt
2nd Eng Bn

6th Division (Kunamoto): LtGen Kuroki Tametomo
11th Inf Bde:
13th & 23rd Inf Regts
12th Inf Bde:
14th & 24th Inf Regts

6th Cav Regt
6th Arty Regt
6th Eng Bn

Note:
For Imperial Guard Div, see text pages 28–29.
  Throughout this text Japanese names are given in their traditional form – family name first, followed by given name.

In 1881, in the military district of Tokyo, a corps of military police – known as Gendarmerie – was organized. From 1888 each of the new territorial divisions had its own unit of Gendarmes, and by 1894 a unit had also been attached to the Imperial Guard Division. Each of these seven military police battalions had 3 companies; all their officers were mounted, while NCOs and rankers mostly served on foot. The Gendarmes were recruited from time-expired NCOs and rankers of the Active Army who had exemplary records. By 1890 military police manpower totalled 1,400, including 700 officers.

Weapons

After having previously employed a wide variety of European and American small arms, in 1880 the IJA adopted as standard the first Japanese-produced rifle – the 11mm M1880 Murata. Modelled partly on the French M1874 Gras, this was a single-shot, bolt-action weapon taking black-powder metal cartridges. The initial model was designated the Type 13 (for the 13th year of the Meiji Emperor's reign). The Type 16 (1883) was a carbine version, and the Type 18 (1885) was a slightly improved modification of the Type 13. The Type 22 (1889) was radically different: now in 8mm calibre, it had an 8-round tubular magazine (5-rd in the carbine version), and fired smokeless ammunition. By 1894 most of the Japanese infantry were equipped with the Type 18, while the Type 22 repeater had been issued to only a few units, notably of the Imperial Guard Division. The old Type 13 was still carried by 1st and 2nd Reserve units.

Until 1890 Japanese cavalrymen were all equipped with lances, but by the outbreak of the First Sino-Japanese War only those of the Imperial

The marching equipment of Japanese line engineers. The sappers at left and right have a pickaxe and a large shovel, respectively, disassembled and with the heads strapped to their knapsacks in leather covers. The central soldier shows, under magnification, the rank of sergeant 1st class; the two shallow upper stripes are in branch-of-service brown, and the broad lower stripe in gold braid is discoloured by the effect of the period photography. Again, the NCO shows a white three-years' service stripe below his ranking. A metal battalion number can just be seen on his brown shoulder straps.

The first Japanese-made modern artillery pieces were the breech-loading M1882 field and mountain guns in 75mm calibre, copied from a Krupp model; this field gun was photographed at the Koishikawa arsenal outside Tokyo. During the war this type equipped two out of the three battalions in each of the IJA's line artillery regiments, the third having mountain guns.

Guard still carried them; line regiments were armed only with sabres (local copies of contemporary European models), and Murata carbines.

Japanese production of modern artillery pieces began in 1882, when a breech-loading 75mm gun was first produced in Osaka. This copy of a Krupp 7.5cm field piece (which itself had been used in Japan since the Satsuma Rebellion) was produced in two versions. The field artillery model was drawn by a four-horse team, while the shorter-barrelled mountain gun, with a lighter carriage, was dismountable for transport in four mule-loads. The IJA formed no heavy artillery units as such, but during 1894–95 it had the following heavy pieces available: 4x 120mm and 12x 90mm guns, plus 8x 150mm and 12x 90mm mortars. Machine guns were introduced only after 1895.

CHINESE ARMIES

By the mid 19th century the 200-year-old Manchurian-descended Qing dynasty ruled over a vast but loosely-governed empire. Between 1851 and 1866 this had been ravaged by a series of ruinously destructive regional uprisings today known collectively as the Taiping Rebellion.[2] The ethnically Manchu government was inefficient, corrupt at every level, and oppressive to various population groups. Its own forces were quite inadequate to win this wave of regional civil wars, and the rebels were only finally crushed by armies raised by local leaders. Thereafter, accepting the realities of the situation, the Beijing government largely devolved administration, security and defence to autocratic regional governors. These leading mandarins funded autonomous military forces from a proportion of the revenues they raised in their provinces, while maintaining rivalrous cliques at the Imperial court. The process of military modernization was slow, piecemeal, and unevenly sustained, since it was carried out almost entirely by some (though not all) of these competitive regional leaders.

By the outbreak of the First Sino-Japanese War the Qing government had started to understand the importance of reforming its central military forces, but the process was only just beginning. Their tactics remained basically defensive, and the majority of the rank-and-file lacked cohesive spirit and were prone to desertion. By contrast, the Imperial Japanese Army was motivated, aggressive, risk-taking, and confident in its modern equipment and training. While there were exceptions, most Chinese units were very unevenly trained, and were led by unprofessional officers who for reasons of pride resented, and therefore ignored, the efforts of foreign instructors. Many instances were reported of Chinese musketeers firing away their ammunition in pointless, noisy displays, but crumbling when they came under accurate enemy fire, and fleeing from infantry contact. A report by the British consul at Tientsin in Zhili province, Henry Bristow, was typical of Western opinions: '[Their military] drill was purely spectacular… for fighting purposes, it was beneath contempt.'

ARMY OF THE EIGHT BANNERS
This was the central military force of the Qing government, descended from the army of Manchu horse-archers which had conquered China

2   See MAA 275, *The Taiping Rebellion 1851–66.*

in 1644. Its name derived from its being structured in eight autonomous 'banners' or corps, each distinguished by a standard of a distinctive colour. Soon after the 17th-century conquest the ranks of this force had been gradually opened to Mongolians and Han Chinese, but in 1894 more than half of its men were still of Manchu background, and 60 per cent of those were still cavalrymen. It then totalled perhaps 250,000 soldiers, who inherited their military profession from their fathers. About half of these were in the north, deployed in or around the capital, Peking (modern Beijing), while the remainder were distributed across Manchuria and Chinese Turkestan, with limited numbers served in the garrisons of provincial cities. It was thus more a 'dynastic' army than a truly national one. The Bannermen dispersed in provincial garrisons usually had inferior training and equipment to those serving in or around Beijing, but the entire organization was militarily conservative. Most of its cavalrymen were horse-archers armed with composite bows, while even those infantrymen who had firearms mostly carried archaic matchlocks.

Magnificent portrait of Hongli, the Qianlong Emperor (r. 1735–96) in full ceremonial armour. The helmet and the silk-covered cuirass, the quiver of arrows for a composite bow slung in a case on the far side, and the horse harness, are all clearly Manchu, showing a strong Mongolian influence. On formal occasions members of the Chinese Imperial Bodyguard were still dressed very similarly to this figure.

On paper, each of the eight Banners was to comprise three divisions (kusai), each made up of 5 battalions (julan), which in turn had 5 companies (niru) of 300 men. In practice, however, the strength of units and sub-units varied widely, so these theoretical multiples of 300/ 1,500/ 7,500 were rarely seen in the field. The divisions might be of either cavalry or infantry; organized on ethnic lines – either Manchu, Mongolian, or Han Chinese – they were commanded by lieutenant-generals. A battalion was commanded by a colonel; a company was a major's command, with a captain for administrative functions, and five NCOs.

Beijing Bannermen

These comprised five elite corps that performed specific duties in and around the Qing capital, plus a central Imperial field army termed the Paid Force. The elite corps were the Imperial Bodyguard, Vanguard Division, Flank Division, Light Division and Firearms Division.

The Imperial Bodyguard were mounted guardsmen selected from among the emperor's own clansmen, responsible for guarding his person and palace. They totalled 3,000 men, equipped with heavy armour and composite bows. The Vanguard Division, consisting of 2,000 Manchu or Mongolian soldiers selected from among the best elements of all the Eight Banners, was tasked with guarding the Forbidden City and with providing the emperor's escort when he travelled. The Flank Division performed duties similar to the Vanguard Division, but had a more junior status; it totalled 4,000 men in 8 battalions of 500, each selected from the best elements in one of the eight Banners. Despite its title, the Light Division consisted of 4,000 soldiers who were trained and equipped to perform siege operations and assaults. The Firearms Division consisted of two categories each with 4,000 soldiers: the Inner units had lighter matchlocks (which were gradually being replaced with modern firearms), while the Outer units had heavier old-fashioned *jingals*, fired from a rest or a wall. The additional Paid Force was a large field army of 60,000 cavalry and 7,000 infantry, which was deployed around Beijing under the direct orders of the emperor. Its name derived from the fact that it was paid more, and more regularly, than any other Chinese military force.

In addition to these corps, the Army of the Eight Banners also included some other special groups. The Foot Force, numbering some 20,000, were a sort of militarized police, responsible for keeping order in the streets and for guarding the walls of Beijing. The Beijing Field Force was established in 1862 around a nucleus of Bannermen who had been trained by the British following the Anglo-French expedition of 1860. With Western-style training and modern firearms, it comprised 6 battalions of 875 infantrymen, two 1,000-man cavalry regiments, and 500 artillerymen who manned 32 smoothbore guns. Frequently, ordinary units of Bannermen were temporarily attached to the Beijing Field Force to receive modern tactical training. Finally, the Tiger-Hunting Battalion was not a true military unit but part of the 'Imperial Hunting Establishment'. Consisting of 4,000 men dressed to resemble tigers, it was formed to accompany the emperor during his tiger-hunts, but it did see action as a military shock-assault force on several occasions during the 19th century.

ARMY OF THE GREEN STANDARD

Distinct from the essentially dynastic Army of the Eight Banners, this other hereditary organization consisted almost entirely of Han Chinese with fewer Manchu or Mongolian soldiers. It was actually made up of 18 autonomous provincial armies, which were raised right across China to perform garrison and security duties and provide a second-line territorial force. Each province had its own local army, which might number from 5,000 up to a maximum of 50,000 according to the population of its home territory. By 1894 the organization totalled some 500,000 infantry and 100,000 cavalry, of three different status-categories: third-class garrison infantry (*shou-ping*); second-class mobile infantry (*pu-ping*); and first-class cavalry (*ma-ping*).

The Army of the Green Standard was organized either in brigades, each consisting of 6 to 8 active battalions plus a depot battalion (and commanded by a colonel), or in regiments of 2 active battalions (commanded by a lieutenant-colonel), but units and sub-units were usually widely dispersed. All the battalions (*ying*) were recruited locally; those of garrison infantry had 2 companies each, and those of mobile infantry 4 to 5 companies. The strength of a single company might vary from 100 men up to a maximum of 400. Each company was commanded by a captain, and could be divided into 2–4 platoons each commanded by a lieutenant. A single platoon was divided into squads of 10–15 soldiers. A cavalry *ying* usually had 2 companies each with 100–125 horsemen.

These fragmented deployment of the Green Standard army was deliberate, since the Qing government feared the assembly of 'private armies' at the disposal of regional warlords. By 1894 the whole organization had more of a constabulary than a military character; it was a major source of patronage, and thus of corruption.

YUNG-YING ARMIES

Since the days of the Opium Wars, the Qing Empire was forced to rely on the creation of volunteer forces (as distinct from the permanent hereditary organizations described above), in order to face foreign interventions and internal rebellions. These temporary armies were made up of *yung* or 'braves', a term indicating volunteers. Although theoretically paid and provisioned by the provincial governments, such forces usually had a quite irregular character. The internal structure of the *Yung-Ying* ('brave battalion') armies was roughly comparable to that of the Army of the Green Standard, with the infantry organized into 500-man 'brave battalions', and the much less numerous cavalry into battalions of about 200.

Over the passage of time the military quality of the Eight Banners and Green Standard armies steadily declined, due to factional rivalries, endemic corruption, and lack of training or modern weapons; meanwhile, that of many 'brave battalions' improved. Their commanders – who came from the provincial elites – often invested large sums to improve their training and to purchase modern firearms from abroad. In practice the modernization of Chinese military forces took place predominantly in the Yung-Ying armies rather than in those of the Eight Banners or Green Standard.

Huai Army

By 1894 the most important of the Yung-Ying forces in existence was the powerful *Huai* Army. This had been created from 1861 onwards by a powerful mandarin named Li Hongzhang, who had first earned promotion for suppressing elements of the Taiping rebels. By the 1890s he was the most prominent figure at the Qing court, and governor of Zhili province surrounding Beijing. He could thus invest large revenues in enlarging and modernizing his armed forces, progressively absorbing the remnants of several other volunteer armies that were disbanded during the second half of the century.

Though recently shorter of funding, by the outbreak of the First Sino-Japanese War the Huai Army totalled some 26,000 men in 52 battalions (of which 7 were mounted, including 3 acting as Li Hongzhang's bodyguard). This innovative leader's forces were mostly armed with modern firearms bought in Shanghai, and unit officers and NCOs were usually chosen for their individual merit. The Huai Army had a significant artillery, consisting of 30 batteries equipped with 7-pdr or 12-pdr Krupp guns. It also included a small *Huai-Yang* riverine force of naval infantry, who manned junks operating on the Yangtze and other rivers.

Armoured guardsman of the Imperial Bodyguard, equipped with composite bow and quiver. At the end of the 19th century traditional archery was still practised on a large scale in the Chinese and Korean armies, being considered as both an art and a fundamental component of military training. (ASKB)

The Qing government had long distrusted the volunteer armies as obvious threats to its authority, but by the 1890s the decline of the Eight Banners and Green Standard armies had forced it to recognize that the Yung-Ying were China's only truly effective forces. By the outbreak of the First Sino-Japanese War they were collectively known as the 'Defence Army', and had taken over most of the Green Standard's military functions. Li Hongzhang saw his Huai Army as the nucleus for a reformed national army, but rivalries between him and other regional magnates prevented him from achieving this. Nevertheless, much of the fighting in 1894 was carried out by his forces, tactically designated the *Beiyang* Army ('Northern Seas Army' – a reference to the region that provided its funding).

Other modernized forces

In 1872 and again in 1876, Li Hongzhang had sent a few of his young officers to Germany to study in the military schools of what was then Europe's leading power. When they returned he was impressed by their standard of military education, and, during the early 1880s, he invited increasing numbers of German instructors to the city of Tientsin. Here German officers organized a special 'instructional corps'; this consisted of 3 battalions of infantry, 2 squadrons of cavalry, and 2 batteries of artillery. In 1885, again in Tientsin, Li Hongzhang founded a German-staffed military academy for the training of future Chinese officers.

Here the cadets learned contemporary Prussian regulations and practices, and became known as the 'model corps'– an allusion to Li Hongzhang's ambition that the graduates should pass on their training throughout the Qing forces. Defeat by the Japanese destroyed Li Hongzhang's influence at court, but between 1895 and the Boxer Rebellion of 1900 the Qing government would authorize the creation of a number of new Yung-Ying forces to be trained and equipped following German models. One of these, the 'Tenacious Army', was the direct heir of the Huai Army disbanded in 1895, and would number 30 battalions led by German instructors..

Weapons

At the time of the First Sino-Japanese War the Chinese forces as a whole were armed with a bewildering variety of different weapons. Most of these were 'traditional' – swords, spears, polearms of many varieties, and composite bows. They were supplemented by large numbers

Guardsman of the Imperial Bodyguard wearing court dress; for colours, compare with Plate D3. The black velvet Manchu *guanmao* hat had a red crown; different coloured balls at the apex, and different feathers hanging behind, followed a formal hierarchy of rank, in which the peacock tail-feather indicated elite status. (ASKB)

of archaic locally-manufactured matchlock muskets, which had originated in 16th-century Portuguese imports.

However, both the Qing government and regional warlords had begun to import modern firearms during the 1850s, and by the 1890s a significant minority of China's forces had European or American rifles. Since these were acquired piecemeal rather than in accordance with any central programme, there were many different models in simultaneous use, including various Enfields, Snider-Enfields, Martini-Henrys, Lee-Metfords, Berdans, Peabody-Henrys, Spencers, Remingtons, Winchesters, Chassepots, Gras and Mausers. This miscellany naturally produced a logistic nightmare, since each model required its own supply of ammunition, and the lack of uniformity might extend to the issue of several different types within a single battalion. In 1876 the Qing government ordered 26,000 11mm single-shot, bolt-action M1871 Mausers, and in 1882 it decided to standardize on them for its regular forces, but this was never achieved. By 1894 the M1871 Mauser was probably the most numerous single type, but many of them were locally-made copies rather than imported from Europe, and their issue was mainly limited to the minority of 'modernized' corps.

The general picture was very similar as regards artillery. Thousands of antique muzzle-loaders made by traditional methods over several centuries co-existed with large numbers of haphazardly-imported modern weapons of varying types, and with locally-made copies of varying quality. The most common were field guns, but some mountain pieces were also acquired. While batteries were far from being homogenous, the most popular imported guns were Krupps and Armstrongs. In 1880 alone, Krupp delivered 149 heavy and 275 field guns; by the beginning of the First Sino-Japanese War the Huai Army had already re-equipped all its batteries with Krupps, making these the most numerous. Chinese troops also deployed a certain number of Gatling, Gardiner, Nordenfeldt and Maxim machine guns, but these seem to have had little effect on the battlefield.

Contemporary drawing showing a Manchu archer of the Army of the Eight Banners; compare with next photo, and with Plate E1. The long pigtail was characteristic of northern China. (ASKB)

KOREAN ARMY

Historically, the territory of Korea was divided into eight provinces, each of which was supposed to maintain a provincial force for security purposes. The provinces were divided into small administrative districts *(hoo)*; each group of ten *hoo* was to provide a single soldier, whose family were to be supported in his absence by the other nine *hoo*. In practice, many exemptions were available, and eventually service could

Photo of a dismounted Manchu horse-archer of the Army of the Eight Banners, showing the composite bow and long-fletched arrows to good effect. In the 1890s most of the Qing regular cavalry consisted of Manchurian or Mongolian horse-archers, who made up about one-third of the entire Eight Banners army.

be avoided altogether by paying a specific tax *(yangyonk)*. The only effective soldiers in the provinces were the sometimes sizeable personal retinues of the regional prefects; however, the *yangyonk* funded a central army based around the royal capital, Seoul. This 'Army of the Five Garrisons' *(Ogunyong)* was to some degree comparable to the Chinese 'Army of the Eight Banners'; however, by 1870 it had become purely ceremonial, and included many free-loading non-combatants.

The first foreign contacts prompted attempts at military reform. During 1871–73 each Korean city was required to raise a garrison company of 120 men, and fortresses were built. An effort to improve the Five Garrisons army culminated in 1881 in its restructuring in two brigades: the Capital Guards Garrison *(Changoyong)* and Palace Guards Garrison *(Muwiyong)*. The abolition of most of the former exemptions from service caused popular discontent, and many soldiers were also angered by the creation of a wholly new and privileged unit. This 200-man Special Skills Force enjoyed better pay and conditions. It was trained with modern weapons by Lt Horimoto Reizo of the Japanese legation guard, and was envisaged as the nucleus for a modernized army. Resentments among the traditional Capital Guards and Palace Guards garrisons led to the 'Imo incident' of July 1882, when conservative mutineers and urban rioters murdered Lt Horimoto and other perceived 'modernizers', and threatened the royal family.

Chinese domination, 1880s

After having to call upon Chinese help to crush this uprising, King Gojong was forced to restore many of the soldiers' former privileges, and to accept Chinese guidance. The Qing officers in Korea reorganized and re-trained the Capital Guards Garrison, which was put under command of the Chinese Gen Yuan Shikai. It was structured in 4 infantry battalions each of 500 men, organized like their Chinese equivalents. The Korean soldiers received modern firearms and training in their use, but their discipline apparently remained questionable. The Palace Guards Garrison was also partly re-trained.

In October 1883, unsatisfied with the progress of modernization, King Gojong decided to invite a US military mission to his country. This did not arrive until 1888, but was then tasked with establishing an academy to train officers and NCOs for a new royal bodyguard. By the end of 1893 the Royal Bodyguard Bn of 500 selected men had been organized, and most of the line units had been re-trained. The Capital Guards Garrison and

Palace Guards Garrison now had two regiments each; a regiment had 3 battalions, each of 4 companies, and each company comprised a captain, a lieutenant, 3 NCOs and 140 rankers. This line army now numbered around 7,000 men, almost entirely infantrymen; there was no separate cavalry corps, and the artillery did not have a stable structure.

Japanese reorganizations, 1896–1907

After the Korean Army failed to put down the Donghak rebellion in southern Korea in June 1894, the pendulum swung back. With the arrival of the Japanese in Seoul, the American military mission ceased its official activities. The Korean regular forces were once again restructured, this time into four 2-battalion brigades (in practice, small regiments) each 800 strong. The new Capital Defence Bde and Infantry Bde were the redesignated Palace Guards Garrison and Capital Guards Garrison, respectively. The new Royal Bodyguard Bde was expanded to the same size, as was the Training Bde; the latter was an entirely new force recruited among south Korean supporters of the Japanese, equipped and trained by the IJA.

After the Japanese victory, the Training Bde was disbanded under pressure from the foreign powers. With their encouragement, in 1896 King Gojong invited in a Russian military mission, but Japanese hostility led to its withdrawal in March 1898. After this episode the Japanese resumed complete control, and reorganized the Korean Army for the last time. By the beginning of 1904 it had 20,000 men, in 2 Guard infantry battalions, 8 of line infantry, one cavalry regiment, and small detachments of artillery and engineers. During the Russo-Japanese War (1904–05) Korea remained formally neutral. In 1907 all its military units were disbanded except for a single Guard battalion, and in 1910 the Kingdom of Korea was annexed to the Empire of Japan.

Print of a matchlock musketeer of the Army of the Eight Banners. The white chest patch bears black characters identifying his unit, and he wears over-trousers or leggings hitched up to a belt under his tunic. In 1884 a European witness estimated that of those Chinese troops issued with any kind of firearms, 50 per cent still had matchlocks, 37.5 per cent had obsolescent Western muzzle-loaders or Chinese-made copies, and only 12.5 per cent modern breech-loaders. (ASKB)

DEFENDERS OF FORMOSA

The island of Formosa (Taiwan) was annexed to the Qing Empire in 1683. Over the next two centuries an increasing number of Chinese settlers arrived on the island, which soon became an important source of rice and camphor. The Chinese settlers, who numbered up to 3 million by 1894, nevertheless had to co-exist uneasily with the large aboriginal population.

These Formosan native communities (see below) were extremely warlike among themselves, and repeatedly resisted Chinese penetrations. By the end of the 19th century only the north and west were under Chinese control, while the central highlands, southern and eastern

Photo of an Eight Banners matchlock musketeer with a relatively light weapon. The 'cartridge' tubes holding black-powder charges for his muzzle-loader are probably made of bamboo, and are carried in cloth pouches around the waist. Note the gun's down-turned 'pistol grip' rather than a buttstock; the inability to fire with the musket properly shouldered would offset any relative accuracy imparted by the long barrel.

areas were still tribal territory. Moreover, the Chinese colonists were also prone to revolt against their own government; and the waters surrounding Formosa were infested by aboriginal pirates. In 1874 a first Japanese expedition was provoked by this piracy, and following this intervention China sent a sizeable number of soldiers in order to complete the conquest of the island. This was never achieved, but the Qing built several coastal batteries with modern European artillery to counter any further foreign incursions. During the Tonkin War (1884–85) the French landed an expeditionary brigade at Keelung in northern Formosa, which destroyed most of these batteries but made little progress inland. From 1886 aboriginal raids against the Chinese settlers became more frequent, and by the arrival of the Japanese Imperial Guard Division at the end of May 1895 the Qing grip on Formosa was already very weak.

Chinese garrison

No regular troops were permanently stationed on Formosa until 1862, when some units of the Army of the Green Standard which had been sent to the island to crush a local rebellion were ordered to remain. Taiwan's unhealthy climate caused serious losses from disease among the soldiers from the mainland, for whom this became an unpopular posting. On paper the garrison was supposed to be 14,000 strong, but disease and desertion had reduced this to just 4,500 by the outbreak of the Tonkin War. Consequently, the garrison from the Green Standard army was supplemented by several corps provided by different Yung-Ying armies in continental China. By 1890 there were 43 of these 'brave battalions' in Formosa, and at least half of these 21,500 troops, including several units provided by the Huai Army, were equipped with modern firearms.

However, in 1894 the Huai Army battalions were shipped home, being replaced by what remained of the so-called 'Black Flag Army'. This had been organized by the warlord Liu Yongfu from 1857, during the chaotic Taiping Rebellion, from among thousands of bandits active on the border between China and Annam (modern Vietnam). Liu Yongfu transformed these gangs into one of China's most effective and best-armed Yung-Ying armies, and was rewarded with the Qing rank of general. His Black Flag mercenaries fought with some success against the French in the Tonkin War. Officially disbanded in 1885, many hundreds of them remained loyal to Liu Yongfu, and followed him when he went to Formosa in August 1894.

At the outbreak of the First Sino-Japanese War there were still 20 Yung-Ying battalions in Formosa. The Qing local governor tried to expand

Korean regular soldiers guarding captured Qing soldiers during the early weeks of the First Sino-Japanese War. For uniform details, compare with Plate G2. The weapons seem to be old percussion muskets imported from the West; large numbers reached Asia in the decades following the American Civil War, and were also copied locally.

his forces by raising new volunteer units in China's Kwantung province, while also sponsoring the creation of local *Hakka* militia units. When the Japanese Imperial Guard Division landed in May/June 1895 the Chinese garrison of the island totalled roughly 50,000 soldiers of various sorts, spread between 200 understrength battalions. When the Republic of Formosa was proclaimed, these Chinese units became the new Formosan Army; however, since they lacked any coherent command structure and often went unpaid, most were rapidly defeated by the Japanese.

Detail from a contemporary engraving depicting a significant moment in the short history of the Republic of Formosa: Chinese commoners from the settler community donate their silver to the new government in Taipei to support the costs of the imminent war. The soldiers at bottom left wear simple turbans, and tabard-like over-jackets with coloured borders and complex identification patches.

Aboriginal forces

From the Chinese viewpoint, Formosa's native population consisted of two distinct elements: the *Hua-hoan* or 'civilized savages', and the *Ya-hoan* or 'wild savages'. The former had submitted to the Chinese, and had

partly lost their original warlike spirit; the latter were still fully independent and pursued their traditional way of life, which included head-hunting. The Ya-hoan comprised eight main tribes: the Ami, Atayal, Bunun, Paiwan, Puyuma, Saisiat, Tsarisen and Tsou. Each of these consisted of several sub-groups or clans, which lived in small villages scattered across the jungle highlands of the interior.

After the first weeks of fighting, the only Chinese who continued to resist were the Black Flags in the south, and small parties from the settler militias. Some of the latter joined forces with the aborigines locally, but since the Ya-hoan had been fighting against the Chinese for centuries their resistance to the Japanese was mostly pursued independently of the Chinese. A few of them took employment with the Japanese as auxiliaries or scouts, but the great majority of tribal warriors resisted the invaders stubbornly.

Detail from a photo of Formosan aborigines. Their partial clothing suggests some contact with the Chinese settlers (see Plate H2), rather than members of the completely untamed *Ya-hoan* tribes. The warriors are armed with light spears and knives; their small dogs were employed for tracking enemies in the jungle as well as for hunting.

SELECT BIBLIOGRAPHY

Abel, Laszlo, 'Japanese Military Modernization and the French Connection', in *Japan Martial Arts Society Newsletter* No.3 (1985)

Bodin, Lynn, *The Boxer Rebellion*, MAA 95 (Osprey Publishing, 1979)

Borton, Hugh, *Japan's Modern Century: From Perry to 1970* (John Wiley & Sons, 1970)

Chartrand, René, *Japanese War Art and Uniforms 1853–1930* (Schiffer Military History, 2011)

Fukushima, Shingo, 'The Building of a National Army' in *Developing Economies* No.3 (1965)

Hacker, B.C., 'The Weapons of the West: Military Technology and Modernization in 19th century China and Japan' in *Technology and Culture* No.18 (1977)

Harries, Meirion & Susie, *Soldiers of the Sun: The Rise and Fall of the Imperial Japanese Army 1868–1945* (Heinemann, 1991)

Heath, Ian, *Armies of the 19th Century – Asia: China* (Foundry Books, 1998)

Heath, Ian, *Armies of the 19th Century – Asia: Japan and Korea* (Foundry Books, 2011)

Jaundrill, D.C., *Samurai to Soldier: Remaking Military Service in Nineteenth-Century Japan* (Cornell University Press, 2016)

Jowett, Philip S., *Imperial Chinese Armies 1840–1911*, MAA 505 (Osprey Publishing, 2016)

Kublin, Hyman, 'The Modern Army of Early Meiji Japan' in *Far Eastern Quarterly* Vol.9 (1949)

Nakanishi, Ritta, *Japanese Military Uniforms 1841–1929: From the Fall of the Shogunate to the Russo-Japanese War* (Dainippon Kaiga Company, 2001)

Olender, Piotr, *Sino-Japanese Naval War 1894–1895* (MMP Books, 2014)

Paine, S.C.M., *The Sino-Japanese War of 1894–1895: Perceptions, Power and Primacy* (Cambridge University Press, 2002)

Paine, S.C.M., *The Japanese Empire: Grand Strategy from the Meiji Restoration to the Pacific War* (Cambridge University Press, 2017)

Powell, Ralph L., *The Rise of Chinese Military Power 1895–1912* (Princeton University Press, 1955)

Presseisen, E.L., *Before Aggression: Europeans Prepare the Japanese Army* (University of Arizona Press, 1975)

Sonoda, Hideiro, 'The Decline of the Japanese Warrior Class 1840–1880' in *Japan Review* Vol.1 (1990)

Wright, Richard N.J., *The Chinese Steam Navy 1862–1945* (Naval Institute Press, 2000)

Yung, Allen, 'Testing the Self-Strengthening: The Chinese Army in the Sino-Japanese War of 1894–95', in *Modern Asian Studies*, Vol. 30, No. 4 (October 1996)

PLATE COMMENTARIES

A: JAPANESE IMPERIAL GUARD DIVISION

The Imperial Japanese Army of 1894 was uniformed according to the dress regulations of 1886; these remained in force until 1904, when the Japanese adopted new khaki uniforms. The austere tunic and small peaked (visored) service cap of the 1886 regulations were influenced by contemporary German military fashions, but the IJA still retained some French elements (e.g. the 'Hungarian knots' of rank embroidered on the sleeves of officers' uniforms). The Imperial Guard Division's uniforms had a number of distinctive features.

A1: Sergeant 1st class, Artillery Brigade

This illustrates the standard dark blue, single-breasted, short-skirted tunic worn by rankers and NCOs of the IJA foot troops. The cap's band and crown-seam piping, the collar and shoulder-strap facings, trouser side-stripes, and forearm rank insignia were all in distinguishing branch-of-service colours. In the Imperial Guard artillery the cap distinctions and all forearm rank stripes were red, while the collar, shoulder straps, edge-piping, and double trouser-stripes were yellow. The Guard infantry had all-red cap, tunic, and trouser distinctions. In the Guard foot branches, both service and parade dress had frontal and bottom edge-piping, in the same colour as the collar and shoulder straps. All ranks wore the brass five-point star cap badge.

The line infantry had yellow cap piping and band, but red collar, shoulder straps, and single narrow trouser stripes; photos sometimes show white metal Arabic unit numerals on the shoulder straps. Line field and garrison artillery had all facings in yellow. Line troops had a separate parade tunic with edge-piping matching the shoulder-strap colours, which was absent from their service dress.

Rank was indicated by number of stripes on each forearm immediately above the straight cuff, extending around the outer surface of the sleeve with a gap on the inside surface. In the Imperial Guard Div all were of the same red facing colour as the cap band; in line units, the deeper NCO stripe was in gold. One shallow coloured stripe identified a private 2nd class; two stripes, private 1st class/ lance corporal; three stripes, corporal; one shallow stripe and one deep NCO stripe, sergeant 2nd class; two shallow stripes and the NCO stripe, sergeant 1st class; and three shallow stripes and the NCO stripe, sergeant-major.

Note: Due to the technical peculiarities of contemporary photography, in the turn-of-the-century photos reproduced in this book most of the branch facing colours show up darker and with much less contrast than in reality.

A2: Captain, 1st Infantry Regiment, summer service dress

Under the 1886 regulations Japanese officers had two uniforms: parade dress, with a double-breasted tunic, and service dress as illustrated here. (For parade dress, see Plate C3.) The service uniform featured this 'patrol jacket', with black silk frontal frogging, loops and edging. It had no shoulder straps or epaulettes, since rank was shown by the black 'Hungarian knots' embroidered above the pointed cuffs; here the three lines of lace forming the knot indicate the rank of captain. The coloured band of the peaked service cap showed the rank group: it had one central line of dark blue piping for company officers, two lines for field officers, and three lines for generals. Sabres were copies of European types.

A3: Corporal, Cavalry Regiment

The 1886 dress regulations prescribed as parade headgear a shako of this type, and it appears in various uniform prints and a few photos, but in practice it was seldom worn except by the Imperial Guard on special occasions. The shako was black for line units, but for the Imperial Guard amaranth-red, with a black leather crown and top and bottom bands. Below a white-over-red tuft, the brass badge was in the form of the Meiji Emperor's distinctive chrysanthemum symbol (note this repeated in red on the valise and saddlebag-cover). The regiment's service cap had a red band and crown piping. Both Guard and line cavalry wore a dark blue 'Attila' jacket; for the Guard this had amaranth-red trefoil shoulder knots, frontal frogging, edging and rank stripes, but a red-piped cavalry-green collar and green side-stripes on the red trousers. The cavalry regiment of the Imperial Guard was the only mounted unit of the IJA that was still equipped with lances in 1894.

Details from a Moritz Rühl plate, 1900, showing a field officer and a company officer of line infantry in parade dress. Both wear gold-trimmed black shakos. Their dark blue double-breasted tunics have red collars (which should show medium and narrow gold braid, respectively, on the top and front edges); red cuffs and frontal piping; gold shoulder straps of double interwoven cords, with star rank insignia; and gold 'Hungarian' sleeve knots. The red trouser stripes differ in width; the sashes are both silver-and-red, but the field officer's has silver tassels, and the company officer's, red.

Part of a Rühl plate showing Japanese cavalry: (1 & 2) Officer and trumpeter of Imperial Guard regiment, both in parade dress; (3 & 4) Officer and trooper of line cavalry, both in service dress. The latter reproduce the green cavalry branch colour of the facings inconsistently; see commentaries to Plates A3 & B2.

B: JAPANESE LINE UNITS

B1: Private 1st class, 6th Infantry Regiment; 3rd Division, First Army, summer

In addition to their standard dark blue uniform, rankers and NCOs of the foot troops were issued an entirely white lightweight uniform for use in hot weather. It is worn here by an infantry private 1st class during the Korean summer 1894 campaign, distinguished only by the infantry-yellow cap band; note that his forearm rank stripes are also in white. It is not uncommon to see in prints the use of the summer cap with the winter uniform, and vice versa; one source states that the Imperial Guard Div's hasty landing on Formosa in summer 1895 was made with the rankers still wearing their dark blue wool uniforms. Officers also had a white summer patrol jacket, complete with white frogging, edging and 'Hungarian knots', but it seems to have been little worn on campaign.

B2: Trooper, 5th Cavalry Regiment; 5th Division, First Army

Line cavalry wore this dark blue 'Attila' jacket and scarlet-red trousers. The cap piping and band, plain jacket collar, shoulder straps, frogging and edging, junior rank stripes and trouser stripe were all in the green cavalry branch colour. The Type 18 Murata carbine was carried slung, with one ammunition pouch on the waist belt. Officers' jackets had black trim, as in other branches.

B3: Gunner, 1st Artillery Regiment; 1st Division, Second Army, winter

While wearing the single-breasted dark blue greatcoat, this line artilleryman shows nothing to distinguish him from an infantryman. Naturally, the greatcoat was much worn during the Manchurian winter, when 1st Div fought on the Liadong Peninsula. Like many, this soldier has acquired or made for himself a sheepskin vest to wear under his coat; some units also made dark blue hoods to add to it. Officers' privately-

purchased greatcoats might be double-breasted and hooded.

The secondary branches of service of the IJA wore distinctive facing colours as follows, on their caps, collars, shoulder straps, shallow rank stripes, and trouser side-stripes: engineers, brown; train, pale blue; intendance, sky blue; medical corps, green; and Gendarmerie, red (see under Plate C3).

C: JAPANESE NAVY & GENDARMERIE

The uniforms worn by the Imperial Japanese Navy in 1894 were those prescribed by the 1883 dress regulations, which were influenced by the British Royal Navy. Like their IJA equivalents, officers of the IJN had two separate uniforms, for parade and service respectively. The parade dress featured a black bicorne hat with a black cockade attached by a gold lace loop; a dark blue double-breasted jacket, with gold epaulettes bearing anchor badges, and a series of gold rank rings around the cuffs; and dark blue trousers with gold side-stripes of differing widths. On the hat, rank was indicated by broad gold edging for flag officers, and broad or narrow silver edging for senior or junior officers respectively. The parade jacket, unlike the service equivalent, was not produced in white for summer wear, but could be worn with white trousers complete with gold side-stripes. For service dress, see under C2.

C1: Seaman, landing party, summer dress

Following the disbandment of the Marine Corps in 1878, sailors among the crews of major IJN warships began to be trained to serve at need in landing parties as naval infantrymen. The naval rankers' blue-trimmed white summer dress shown here was worn with a simple straw hat displaying a 'cap tally' with gold-yellow script, and anchor badges on the tails; the dark blue winter dress included a round, peakless sailor's cap. Gaiters under the trousers were used, like the rifle equipment, only when going ashore.

C2: Senior petty officer

Senior petty officers wore this British-style double-breasted jacket for winter service dress, complete with buttons around the outside of the cuffs. The officers' superior-quality service dress cap had a gold band and frontal badge, and different rank groups were distinguished by the dimensions of the badge and varying patterns in the weave of the gold band. Their dark blue single-breasted service jacket had edging in black mohair around the collar and pockets, and forming a series of rank rings around the cuffs. Entirely dark blue trousers were worn over black shoes. Their summer service dress was entirely white, including the elements that were in black mohair on the winter uniform. The senior petty officers' uniform was also made in a white version for hot weather.

C3: Major, Gendarmerie, parade dress

This army staff officer of the elite military police, coming aboard a capital ship to confer with the admiral's staff, exemplifies the double-breasted uniform worn by IJA officers on parade. The Gendarmerie shako, unlike that of line units, was red with a black bottom band, bearing the Imperial chrysanthemum badge. The number and dimensions of the gold piping identified rank: a major had four lines of narrow piping around the base of the band. The dark blue double-breasted tunic had a red collar and cuffs, as on this branch's service tunic, with the collar and front edge piped in gold.

For other regimental line officers the branch-colour collar had gold braid edging on the top and front according to the rank group: field officers had wide braid, and company officers medium braid. Interwoven gold-cord shoulder straps, on a branch-colour base, were of triple lace for field officers, and double lace for company officers. Exact rank was identified by the number of five-point stars applied to them: 3, 2 and 1 for colonels down to majors, and 1 for all company grades. The 'Hungarian knots' of rank on the forearms were like those on the service dress, but in gold rather than black: 6, 5 and 4 lines for field officers, and 3, 2 and 1 for company officers. Gendarmerie officers wore a tasselled waist-sash striped in gold and the collar branch colour. Red trousers were worn with differing widths of black side-stripes.

In parade dress, rankers of the Gendarmerie also wore a red shako with black bottom band; the standard tunic, with red collar, shoulder straps, and straight red cuffs; and red trousers with a narrow black side-stripe. Their service dress cap was dark blue with red piping and band; the tunic had a red collar and shoulder straps and plain dark blue cuffs, but they wore the same red trousers as for parade dress.

D: CHINA: BEIJING BANNERMEN

Until 1895, with the exception of a few and temporary 'Westernized' corps, Chinese armies did not wear true uniforms. Their dress was usually brightly coloured, and some regional variations made it possible to identify the soldiers' ethnic origins. Manchurians and Mongolians were dressed quite similarly, in clothing of a more austere cut, while Han Chinese usually wore looser-fitting tunics made of cotton or silk. Tunics were made in many different colours, and usually had edging-bands in a contrasting colour. The various units that made up the Beijing Bannermen presented a wide variety of such costumes.

D1: Swordsman, Tiger-Hunting Battalion
The most flamboyant costume was worn by the Tiger-Hunters, who were employed as fanatical assault troops and skirmishers in 19th-century Qing armies. Their clothing was designed to imitate a tiger, with a separate headpiece apparently made on a bamboo frame. The members of this battalion were all equipped as swordsmen, and carried strikingly decorated round, convex bamboo shields.

D2: Rifleman, Inner units, Firearms Division
The ultimate contrast is provided by the modernized appearance of these units. The soldier's round cap, pullover tunic and trousers are locally-made, but present a Western silhouette. Since the 1850s it had become increasingly common for Imperial troops to display on chest and back a light-coloured disc bearing characters identifying the unit, often by a commander's name. The black boots and belt equipment are clearly European imports, as is the weapon – a British 303in Lee-Metford magazine rifle purchased in Shanghai (here, probably an 1889 Mk I, firing black-powder cartridges).

D3: Guardsman, Imperial Bodyguard
The elite soldiers of the Imperial Bodyguard were all equipped as mounted archers in the traditional style of the Manchus,

and their main weapon was the powerful composite bow of the Asian steppes. While on active service they usually wore helmets and full armour (see Plate G1), but might discard them while guarding the emperor in his palace. The guardsman's status is marked by the single peacock tail-feather hanging from his black Manchu hat, and his magnificently woven and embroidered silk outer robe, showing cloud motifs, is of Mongolian style.

E: CHINA: HEREDITARY & VOLUNTEER ARMIES
E1: Manchu horse-archer, Army of the Eight Banners
The costumes worn by the hereditary Army of the Eight Banners were extremely traditional. Its majority of cavalry were raised in Manchuria and Mongolia, though it also included Chinese infantry. This Manchu mounted archer wears a loose, flowing robe of a type common to both the former peoples; he is identified by his distinctive hat, since Mongolian soldiers usually wore fur-lined caps.

Rühl images of a Japanese sergeant 1st class of engineers in service dress, and a captain of the train (logistics) corps in parade dress.

(Left) All dark blue uniform, with the engineers' brown branch colour displayed on cap band and piping, collar, shoulder straps (obscured here), trouser-stripe, and forearm rank stripes. In the latter, note that the two shallow brown stripes appear separately, above and below what by regulation should be a broad gold NCO stripe. A photo of an engineer NCO (see page 31) shows the conventional arrangement of rank stripes.

(Right) The black shako and dark blue double-breasted tunic have gold lace and insignia; the train's branch colour of light blue appears on the collar, cuffs, frontal piping, and the trouser stripe; the silver-and-red sash has red tassels.

Chinese swordsman of the Army of the Green Standard; in this print the unbordered tunic, the trousers and the over-trousers are all of different solid colours, and are cut fairly closely. The headgear is a bamboo sun hat with decorative painted apex and border. Compare the bamboo shield with Plate H1. (ASKB)

E2: Musketeer, Army of the Green Standard
The provincially-raised units of the Army of the Green Standard also inherited their profession from their fathers. Locally enlisted to serve as dispersed garrison troops under commanders drawn from provincial elites, by 1894 they had become more of a constabulary than a military organization. They were nearly all Han Chinese, so dressed quite similarly – although this man wears a Manchu hat, rather than the simple turban with hanging ends which was more typically Chinese. Turbans and tunics were of many different colours, often of bright shades, and the latter were typically edged with sometimes decorative bands in contrasting colours. The use of loose over-trousers suspended at the waist was quite common, as were felt boots. Only a minority had firearms, and those that did carried matchlock muskets. These continued to be manufactured, as did several odd composite weapons. The example illustrated copies some external elements of a Western rifle; however, its short, angular buttstock is traditional, and the bamboo powder-cartridges worn around the waist confirm that it is a muzzle-loader. The overall quality of this soldier's appearance suggests that he belongs to a unit of mobile infantry (*pu-ping*) rather than the very basic garrison infantry.

E3: Volunteer, *Huai* Army
Although the 'brave battalions' of this leading *Yung-Ying* army created by Li Hongzhang enjoyed modern weapons and training, they were dressed largely in Chinese fashion.

This 'brave's' black Manchu hat, and his hair dressed in a long pigtail, are typical of northern China, where most of these soldiers were being recruited by the 1890s. The dark blue silk tunic, with red decorative edging, is shorter than usual, which suggests some Western influence. On the chest (and the back) is a white identification patch of the most modern type, now bearing the soldier's personal number as well as his unit identity; in 'brave battalions' the latter might be written in boastful terms.The black belt equipment has been imported from Germany, together with the 11mm Mauser M1871 rifle.

F: CHINA: 'NEWLY CREATED ARMY' & *BEIYANG* FLEET
F1: Infantry NCO, Newly-Created Army
While this modernized volunteer force played no part in the First Sino-Japanese War, its inclusion may be justified by the fact that it was authorized and created immediately afterwards, before the end of 1895. Originally titled the 'Pacification Army', it soon came under the command of the ambitious Gen Yuan Shikai, and by the end of the year it boasted 5 infantry battalions, 4 cavalry troops, 3 artillery battalions, and 6 engineer companies. The uniform was similar to that of the former *Beiyang* Fleet (see F2), and included a black Manchu hat with both a black and a white feather hanging at the back. The collar of the dark blue single-breasted tunic had black edging and inset piping. Above the black cuffs, according to rank, non-commissioned officers displayed a gold stripe and other elements. The trousers were white, worn tucked into locally-made boots. Officers had a much more elaborate tunic, with gold edging and decorative embroidery on the collar, gold shoulder cords and 'Hungarian knots' indicating rank, and displayed rank-specific numbers of red stripes on black trousers. This 'brave's' weapon is the German 7.92mm M1888 'Commission rifle', with a fixed box magazine which took *en bloc* 5-round clips of smokeless ammunition. Imported in great numbers, in 1895 it began local production at the Hanyang arsenal.

F2: Officer, *Beiyang* Fleet
Unlike China's other regional navies, whose crews were dressed like the foot troops of the Army of the Green Standard, the elite northern fleet had uniforms. The officers wore a black Manchu hat with a thoroughly modernized uniform which echoes that of F1. The dark blue single-breasted tunic had black collar edging and piping; extensive black decorations on the shoulders, torso, and skirt edges; and, above the blue cuffs, a gold stripe and decorative designs which varied according to rank.

F3: Marine, *Beiyang* Fleet
Each of this fleet's major warships had a contingent of naval infantrymen, who were dressed and equipped like this striking figure. The headgear is a wide-brimmed straw hat of European style. The red single-breasted tunic, worn with matching trousers, has a black collar, cuff and skirt edging, and torso decorations. The rifle is, again, a single-shot 11m Mauser M1871, imported complete with its bayonet.

G: KOREAN ARMY

G1: Guardsman, Royal Bodyguard

Until the arrival of a Russian military mission in 1896–97 the Korean Army had no uniforms to speak of, since its members were dressed in traditional costume. King Gojong's Royal Bodyguard still wore these helmets and silk-covered armour in Qing fashion, and were armed with composite bows. Until 1894 most officers of the Army of the Five Garrisons were also dressed and equipped like this figure; most of them were mounted, although the army did not have cavalry units until 1903–04.

G2: Rifleman, Capital Guards Garrison

The general appearance of Korean soldiers at the end of the 19th century was simpler and less various than that of their Chinese contemporaries, but included several distinctive elements. One was this *gat* headgear, characterizd by a cylindrical crown and wide brim, and made from black horsehair on a bamboo frame. The stripes of red cloth wrapped around it bore the unit's name in black characters. Black and dark blue were the most common colours for Korean military dress; this loosely-cut, single-breasted black tunic has broad red edging at the neck and the very wide cuffs, and is worn with distinctively Korean baggy white trousers. His rifle is a single-shot 10.75mm M1870 Russian Berdan II, complete with its cruciform socket bayonet.

G3: Archer, Palace Guards Garrison

The Palace Guards Garrison, tasked with protecting King Gojong's palace and person, enjoyed a number of privileges compared with other Korean soldiers. This man wears another type of traditional wide-brimmed hat painted black; it differs from the *gat* in being made of straw, with a domed crown, and, for this unit, a red button at the apex with red streamers, and two upright feathers. The long robe is in red, the distinctive colour of the Palace Guards Garrison. He carries a high-quality sword as well as his composite bow and its quiver.

H: DEFENDERS OF FORMOSA

H1: Standard-bearer, Formosan Republican Army

This was an extremely heterogeneous force, comprising mainland Chinese troops from the Green Standard and *Yung-Ying* armies, local *Hakka* militias recruited from the Chinese settlers, and sometimes associated aboriginal war-parties. This Chinese soldier, probably shipped over from Kwantung, bears the national flag of the very short-lived Republic of Formosa. He would have a slung sword, and carries a round bamboo shield decorated in the traditional Chinese way with the painted face of a sacred animal (here the tiger, echoing that on the flag) or a deity.

H2: Warrior, *Hua-hoan* tribes

The so-called 'civilized savages' of northern Formosa usually wore sleeveless jackets and short kilt-like skirts. This warrior carries a typical long, slightly curved knife or shortsword at his waist. He is blowing on the smouldering end of a match-cord before fitting it to the cock of his light matchlock musket. An archaic weapon acquired from the Chinese settlers, this has a typical down-curved pistol-grip in place of a buttstock, and lacks either a trigger-guard or a pan-cover. His simple bag contains bamboo cartridges

The costume of this infantryman, also probably from a Green Standard force, is more loosely cut and the tunic has white borders; the identification disc gives more information, as was also the case in the *Yung-Ying* armies. A wide variety of traditional polearms might be carried by Green Standard infantry; this slim 'bill' is essentially a sword-blade mounted on a staff, while others included spears, spikes, tridents, and variously shaped 'halberds'. (ASKB)

with measured powder charges, and probably his food rations for a day or two.

H3: Warrior, *Ya-hoan* tribes

By contrast, the 'wild savages' of central and southern Formosa fought almost naked, and lacked virtually any firearms. Rudimentary helmets, cuirasses and shields were all made from hard bamboo. Offensive weapons included clubs, spears, longbows, slings, swords and knives; since metals were extremely scarce on the island, many of the latter were made of various hardwoods. The extra-long club or 'halberd' carried by this Ami warrior was known as a *papalo*, and its shape suggests that it may have been inspired by some kind of Chinese billhook. It was made of laboriously-carved hardwood, and had an extremely sharp diamond-section blade.

INDEX